WHEN THINGS FELL APART

In the later decades of the twentieth century, Africa plunged into chaos. States failed, governments became predators, and citizens took up arms. In *When Things Fell Apart*, Robert H. Bates advances an explanation of state failure in Africa. In so doing, he plumbs the depths of the continent's late-century tragedy, the logic of political order, and the foundations of the state. This book covers a wide range of territory by drawing on materials from Rwanda, Sudan, Liberia, and Congo. Written to be accessible to the general reader, it is nonetheless a must-read for scholars and policymakers concerned with conflict and state failure.

Robert H. Bates has conducted field work in Zambia, Sudan, Uganda, Kenya, Colombia, and Brazil. Before coming to Harvard, he held faculty appointments at the California Institute of Technology and Duke University and worked as a researcher at the Institute of Development Studies at the University of Nairobi, the Institute for Social Research at the University of Zambia, and Fedesarrollo in Bogota, Colombia. Bates currently serves as a researcher and resource person with the Africa Economic Research Consortium, Nairobi; as a member of the Political Instability Task Force of the United States government; and as Professeur Associe, School of Economics, University of Toulouse, where he has taught since 2000. Among his most recent books are *Analytic Narratives* with Avner Greif and colleagues (1999), *Prosperity and Violence* (2001), *Beyond the Miracle of the Market, Second Edition* (2005), and *The Political Economy of Economic Growth in Africa, 1960–2000* (2 vols.) with Benno Ndulu and colleagues (2007).

When Things Fell Apart

State Failure in Late-Century Africa

Robert H. Bates

Harvard University

CAMBRIDGE
UNIVERSITY PRESS

University Printing House, Cambridge CB2 8BS, United Kingdom

One Liberty Plaza, 20th Floor, New York, NY 10006, USA

477 Williamstown Road, Port Melbourne, VIC 3207, Australia

314-321, 3rd Floor, Plot 3, Splendor Forum, Jasola District Centre, New Delhi - 110025, India

103 Penang Road, #05-06/07, Visioncrest Commercial, Singapore 238467

Cambridge University Press is part of the University of Cambridge.

It furthers the University's mission by disseminating knowledge in the pursuit of education, learning and research at the highest international levels of excellence.

www.cambridge.org
Information on this title: www.cambridge.org/9781107569805

First published 2008
Reprinted 2008, 2009 (twice)
Canto Classics edition 2015

A catalogue record for this publication is available from the British Library

ISBN 978-1-107-56980-5 Paperback

To my mentors

Harvey Glickman
Haverford College

Martin Kilson
Harvard University

Richard Sklar
University of California, Los Angeles

Thayer Scudder
California Institute of Technology

Contents

Contents

Part Four
Appendix

Acknowledgments

Working in Uganda in the early 1980s, I came to learn what it meant to live in a world of violence. Among the reasons my colleagues in the Ministry of Cooperatives welcomed the overthrow of Idi Amin was that with Uganda no longer a pariah state, they could now attend international conferences. And among the reasons they attended such conferences was that they could then sleep, for they need not fear the arrival of soldiers in the night. Insights like this reminded me of something of which I was but fleetingly aware: not only the fragility of life, but also its political premise. I knew then that I would some day have to return to the issues to which that recognition gave rise.

To gain a respite from the tensions of working amidst violence, I turned instead to the study of the international coffee industry. To write up my research into the coffee industry, I spent a sabbatical year at the Center for Advanced Study in Palo Alto, California. Research in Colombia had quickly taught me that conflict was not a phenomenon confined solely to Africa.

Acknowledgments

I was therefore fortunate that Avner Greif was also in residence and that we could ponder together the roots of political order. The model that Avner, Smita Singh, and I produced underpins this work.

While I was laboring in archives in Latin America and at the Center for Advanced Study in California, governments in Africa were being overthrown by political reformers and decimated by political insurgents. When I returned to the study of Africa, I therefore had much ground to make up. Backed by funding from the Institute for International Development (HIID) at Harvard University, I assembled a collection of books and articles and, in conjunction with scholars from the African Economic Research Consortium (AERC), began a collaborative study of economic growth on the continent. I wish to acknowledge the support of Dwight Perkins and Jeffrey Sachs at HIID and that of my colleagues at AERC: Jean-Paul Azam, Paul Collier, Augustin Fosu, Jan Willem Gunning, Benno Ndulu, Dominique Nijinkeu, Stephen O'Connell, and the skilled stalwarts of the Secretariat.

A superb team of students made this study possible. I salute in particular the contributions of Karen Ferree and Smita Singh, who helped to launch it. Marc Alexander, James Habyarimana, Matthew Hindman, and Macartan Humphreys made major contributions. I wish also to thank Daron Haddass, Andy Harris, Kusisami Hornberger, Olivia Lau, Rebecca Nelson, Maria Petrova, Naunihal Singh, and Tsvetana Petrova.

Acknowledgments

Thanks to Nahomi Ichino and James Robinson for reading and commenting on earlier drafts, as well as members of Gov. 2227: Andrew Beath, Matthew Blackwell, Ryan Bubb, Deepa Dhume, Daniel Fetter, Amanda Garrett, Andy Harris, Jennifer Howk, Janet Lewis, Christopher Rhodes, Anna Vodopyanov, Jacqueline Jansen, and Subhasish Ray. Thanks, too, to the three superb readers, selected by Lewis Bateman and Margaret Levi. I have benefited from comments made by participants at seminars at Yale University, Stanford University, the California Institute of Technology, the University of Oxford, Harvard University, the Peace Research Institute in Oslo, and the Rockefeller Foundation's villa in Belagio; at the annual meetings of the Political Science and Economic History Associations; and at workshops in the Kenya Institute for Policy Research and Analysis and the Africa Economic Research Consortium in Nairobi. I am particularly grateful to the Division of Humanities and Social Sciences at Caltech for appointing me as a Moore Fellow, thus giving me the time to launch this book. Special thanks, too, to the Economics Faculty at Toulouse University, especially to Jean-Paul Azam and Bruno Biais, with whom I have shared many of the ideas that worked their way into my argument.

This project has been supported by the Center for International Development and the Weatherhead Center for International Affairs at Harvard University; by a Clark Fellowship from the office of the Dean of the Faculty of Arts and Sciences,

Acknowledgments

Harvard University; and by the Africa Economic Research Consortium. Funding from the United States Institute for Peace (Grant No. USIP-0259750), the Carnegie Corporation, and the National Science Foundation (Grant No. SES-09905568) brought the project to completion.

I wish as well to acknowledge the impact upon my thinking of the members of the Political Instability Task Force, in particular David Epstein and Jack Goldstone.

I dedicate this book to my mentors: those whose counsel eased my entry into this profession and whose scholarship has inspired my own.

Portions of this study have previously appeared in the following publications and are employed with permission of the publishers:

Bates, R. H. (2006). "Institutions and Development," *Journal of African Economies* 15(1): 10–61.

Bates, R. H. (Forthcoming). State Failure: A Model with Tests from African Data. In *Political Violence*. Edited by Tarek Masoud and Stathis Kalyvas. New Haven, CT: Yale University Press.

Bates, Robert, Avner Greif, and Smita Singh (2004). Tribal Societies. In *Politics from Anarchy to Democracy: Rational Choice in Political Science*. Edited by Morris Irwin, Joe Oppenheimer, and Karol Edward Soltan. Stanford, CA: Stanford University Press.

Ndulu, B., P. Collier, et al. (2007). *The Political Economy of Economic Growth in Africa, 1960–2000*. Vol. 1. Cambridge, U.K.: Cambridge University Press.

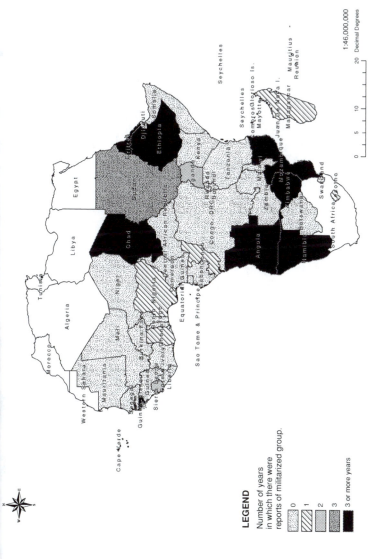

Reported presence of military groups, 1970–1974. Map compiled by Doran Haadass from data collected by the research team. Countries with white background were not included in the sample for which data were collected.

LEGEND

Number of years
in which there were
reports of militarized group.

0
1
2
3
3 or more years

1:46,000,000

0   5   10   20   Decimal Degrees

Part One

Introduction

1

Introduction

I n late-century Africa, things fell apart. By way of illustration, consider Figure 1.1, which lists civil wars in African countries from 1970 to 1995, as judged by the World Bank.

As time passes, the list grows. Angola, Chad, Namibia, Nigeria, and Sudan enter the 1970s war-torn; in the mid-1970s, Sudan exits the list, but Equatorial Guinea and Zimbabwe join it; by 1980, Zimbabwe departs from the ranks of the war-torn, but is replaced by Mozambique, Nigeria, and Uganda. The pattern – a few dropping off, a larger number entering in – continues into the early 1990s. Only one country that was conflict ridden in 1990 becomes peaceful by 1992, while eleven others crowd into the ranks of Africa's failed states.

Humanitarians, policymakers, and scholars: Each demands to know why political order gave way to political conflict in late-century Africa. Stunned by the images and realities of political disorder, I join them in search of answers. In so doing, I – a political scientist – turn to theories of the state and

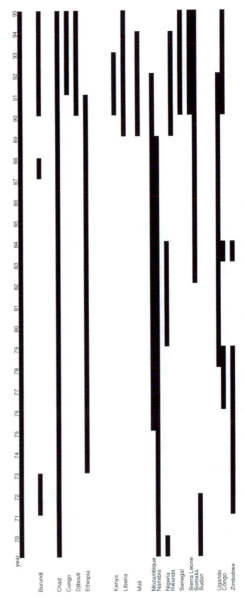

Figure 1.1. Civil wars, Africa 1970–1995. *Source:* World Bank (Sambanis 2002).

locate the sources of political disorder midst the factors that lead states to break down.

I anchor this book in the work of Weber (1958) and view coercion as the distinctive property of politics. As will become clear in the next chapter, I depart from Weber – and his "structuralist" descendants[1] – by turning to the theory of games. Driven by the realities of Africa, I view political order as problematic: In light of the evidence Africa offers, political order *cannot* be treated as a given. Rather, I argue, it results when rulers – whom I characterize as "specialists in violence" – choose to employ the means of coercion to protect the creation of wealth rather than to prey upon it and when private citizens choose to set weapons aside and to devote their time instead to the production of wealth and to the enjoyment of leisure.[2] When these choices constitute an equilibrium, then, I say, political order forms a state.[3]

To address the collapse of political order in late-century Africa, I therefore return to theory – the theory of the state – and to theorizing – the theory of games. I do so because proceeding in this fashion points out the conditions under which political order can persist – or fail. I devote Chapter 2 to an informal

---

[1] Evans, P., T. Skocpol, and D. Rueschmeyer (1985), *Bringing the State Back In*, Cambridge, U.K.: Cambridge University Press provides perhaps the best-known example.

[2] I am drawing on Bates, R. H., A. Greif, et al. (2002), "Organizing Violence," *Journal of Conflict Resolution* 46(5): 599–628.

[3] The ambiguous phrasing is intended.

Introduction

derivation of those conditions. In the remaining chapters, I turn from deduction to empirics and explore the extent to which these conditions were to be found, or were absent, in late-century Africa. The evidence leads me to conclude that in the 1980s and 1990s, each of three key variables departed from the levels necessary to induce governments and citizens to choose in ways that would yield political order.

The Literature

Following the outbreak of conflict in Serbia, Somalia, Rwanda, and elsewhere, the study of political violence has once again become central to the study of politics. Familiar to many, for example, would be the attempts by Collier and Hoeffler (2004) and Fearon and Laitin (2003) to comprehend the origins of civil wars. Also familiar would be studies of the impact of ethnicity (Fearon and Laitin 2003), democracy (Hegre, Gates et al. 2001; Hegre 2003), and natural-resource endowments (e.g., Ross 2004). In my attempts to comprehend why things fell apart in late-century Africa, I draw upon these writings. But I also take issue with them, for virtually all share common properties from which I seek to depart.

Consider, for example, the assumption that civil war can be best treated as the outcome of an insurgency. When thinking about the origins of political disorder in Africa, I can find no way of analyzing the origins of insurrection without starting with the behavior of governments. The conditions that led to the breakdown of order in Africa include the authoritarian nature of its states and their rulers' penchant for predation. By rendering their people insecure, they provoked insurgencies. While both insurrectionaries and incumbents must necessarily feature in the analysis of political disorder, in this instance it makes sense not to focus exclusively on the rebels but to stress as well the behavior of those whom they seek to drive from power.

Recent contributions exhibit a second common feature: the methods that they employ. Utilizing cross-national data, they apply statistical procedures to isolate and measure the relationship of particular variables with the onset and duration of civil wars. I, too, make use of cross-national data; but rather than collecting data for all countries in the globe, I restrict my efforts to Africa. I do so in part because Africa provides an unsettling range of opportunities to explore state failure and because political disorder is so important a determinant of the welfare of the continent. I also do so because I find it necessary to draw upon my intuition. To employ that intuition, I need first to inform it, be it by immersing myself in the field or in qualitative accounts set down by observers. I have therefore made use of a selected set of cases – those from the continent of Africa – and my knowledge of their politics.[4]

---

[4] The use of a subset of countries also eases the search for exogenous variables, and thus causal analysis. For example, given the small size of Africa's

Introduction

Lastly, if only because they are based on the analysis of cross-national data, contemporary studies exhibit a third property: Their conclusions take the form of "findings." These findings are based upon relationships between a selection of key variables and the outbreak or duration of civil wars. Collier and Hoeffler (2004), for example, stress the importance of "opportunities," that is, chances to secure economic rewards and to finance political organizations. Noting that the magnitude of primary product exports, the costs of recruiting, and access to funding from diasporas relate to the likelihood of civil war, they conclude that "economic viability appears to be the predominant systematic explanation of rebellion" (p. 563). Fearon and Laitin (2003), by contrast, conclude that "capabilities" play the major role: "We agree that financing is one determinant of the viability of insurgency," they write (p. 76). But they place major emphasis on "state administrative, military, and police capabilities" (p. 76), measures of which bear significant relationships to the outbreak of civil wars in their global set of data.

In this work, I proceed in a different fashion. I start by first capturing the logic that gives rise to political order. While I, too, test hypotheses about the origins of disorder, I derive

economies, I can treat global economic shocks as exogenous – something that yields inferential leverage when seeking to measure the impact of economic forces on state failure.

Introduction

these hypotheses from a theory. By adopting a more deductive approach, I depart from the work of my predecessors.

Key Topics

Energized by such works as Kaplan's "The Coming Anarchy" (1994), students of Africa have focused on the relationship between ethnic diversity and political conflict. At least since the time that William Easterly and Ross Levine penned "Africa's Growth Tragedy" (1997), empirically minded social scientists have sought to capture the impact of ethnicity on the economic performance of Africa's states. Interestingly, however, they have found it difficult to uncover systematic evidence of the relationship between measures of ethnicity and the likelihood of political disorder.[5]

In this study I, too, find little evidence of a systematic relationship. And yet, the qualitative accounts – be they of the killing fields of Darfur or of the tenuous peace in Nigeria – continue to stress the central importance of ethnicity to political life in Africa. In response, I argue that ethnic diversity does not cause violence; rather, ethnicity and violence are joint

---

[5] For a discussion, see Bates, R. H., and I. Yackolev (2002), Ethnicity in Africa, in *The Role of Social Capital In Development*, edited by C. Grootaert and T. van Bastelaer, New York: Cambridge University Press; and Fearon, J., and D. Laitin (2003), "Ethnicity, Insurgency and Civil War," *American Political Science Review* 97(1): 75–90.

products of state failure. Their relationship is contingent: It occurs when political order erodes and politicians forge political organizations in the midst of political conflict.

The political significance of resource wealth has also attracted much attention. Analyzing their data on civil wars, Collier and Hoeffler (2004) report that "dependence upon primary commodity exports" constituted "a particularly powerful risk factor" for the outbreak of civil war (p. 593). Africa is, of course, noted for its bounteous natural endowments of petroleum, timber, metals, and gemstones. And scholars and policymakers have documented the close ties between the diamond industry and UNITA (National Union for the Total Independence of Angola) in Angola (Fowler 2000), the smuggling of gemstones and the financing of rebels in Sierra Leone (Reno 2000), and the mining of coltan and the sites of rebellion in eastern Zaire (present-day Democratic Republic of the Congo) (Kakwenzire and Kamukama 2000).

And yet, using Collier and Hoeffler's (2004) own data, Fearon (2005) has demonstrated that their findings are fragile, depending in part on decisions about how to measure and classify cases. In this study, too, I fail to find a significant relationship between the value of natural resources and the likelihood of state failure.[6] Once again, then, there arises

---

[6] For both Fearon (2005) and myself (this work), only the value of petroleum deposts is related to political disorder. Even here the relationship is fragile, however.

a disparity between the evidence from cross-national regressions and that from qualitative accounts. I shall argue that the disparity suggests that the exploitation of natural resources for war finance is a correlate rather than a cause of political disorder.

A third factor plays a major role in the literature: democratization. Qualitative accounts, such as those of Mansfield and Snyder (Mansfield and Snyder 1995; Snyder 2000) suggest that democratization produces political instability and leads to the mobilization of what Zakaria (1997) calls "illiberal" political forces. Careful empirical researchers, such as Hegre (Hegre, Gates et al. 2001; Hegre 2004), confirm that new democracies and intermediate regimes – those lying somewhere between stable authoritarian and consolidated democratic governments[7] – exhibit significantly higher rates of civil war. As demonstrated by Geddes (2003), many of these intermediate regimes are the product of the "third wave" of democratization (Huntington 1991) and the collapse of communist regimes and are therefore themselves new and vulnerable to disorder.

In the 1980s and 1990s, many of Africa's governments reformed. Regimes that once had banned the formation of political parties now faced challenges at the polls from

---

[7] Using Polity coding. Available online at: http://www.cidcm.umd.edu/polity/.

candidates backed by an organized political opposition. And in the late 1980s and early 1990s, militias assembled, states failed, and Africa faced rising levels of political disorder. The experience of Africa thus appears to conform to what the literature has recorded: Electoral competition and state failure go together.

In analyzing the impact of political reform, I employ two measures: the movement from military to civilian rule and the shift from no- or one- to multiparty systems. In discussions of democracy, the followers of Schumpeter (1950) argue for the sufficiency of party competition; those of Dahl (1971) contend that party competition is necessary but not sufficient. Without an accompanying bundle of political and civil rights, the latter argue, contested elections are not of themselves evidence of democratic politics. In debates over the relationship between party systems and democracy, I concur with the followers of Dahl. When addressing political reform, I pay no attention to the number of political parties, their relative vote shares, or the conditions under which the opposition is allowed to campaign. I therefore address not the relationship between democracy and political conflict but rather the relationship between political reform and political disorder.

Lastly, there are those who emphasize the impact of poverty. That poverty and conflict should go together is treated as noncontroversial, as if disorder were simply an expected corollary of the lack of economic development.[8] But consider: If, as many argue, lower per capita incomes imply lower wages and therefore lower costs of rebellion, so too do they imply fewer gains from predation; income thus cancels out the ratio between the costs and benefits. From the theoretical point of view, moreover, there is simply little that can be said about the relationship between the average level of income – or, for that matter, poverty – and incentives for violence. As I will argue in Chapter 2, for our purposes, discussions of private income can be set aside; for the logic of political order suggests that the focus be placed not on *private* income but rather on *public* revenues. Economic shocks will indeed play a major role in this analysis, but the focus will be on their impact on the revenues of states, not on the incomes of individuals.[9] In this work, when I measure the impact of income per capita, I treat it as a control variable, rather than as a variable of theoretical interest.

In Chapter 2, I parse the logic of political order. I recount the theory informally, portraying the interaction between governments and citizens and among citizens as well. Presented as a

---

[8] Indeed, see Sambanis, N., and H. Hegre (2006), "Sensitivity Analysis of Empirical Results on Civil War Onset," *The Journal of Conflict Resolution* 50(4): 508–35. The authors point to per capita income as one of the very few variables that bears a robust relationship with civic violence.

[9] See the arguments in Hirshleifer, J. (1995), Theorizing About Conflict, in *Handbook of Defense Economics*, edited by K. Hartley and T. Sandler, New York: Elsevier.

Introduction

fable, the argument is based upon rigorous foundations and points to the conditions under which governments choose to engage in predation and citizens choose to take up arms.[10]

Chapters 3 through 5 set out the conditions that prevailed prior to the collapse of political order. They document the social and political configurations that were in place at the time of the impact of the economic and political shocks that dismantled the state in Africa. In Chapter 6, states fracture and political disorder engulfs nations in Africa. Chapter 7 concludes.

[10] The informed reader will note the parallels between my analysis and that of Azam, J.-P., and A. Mesnard (2003), "Civil War and the Social Contract," *Public Choice* 115(3–4): 455–75; Snyder, R., and R. Bhavani (2005), "Diamonds, Blood and Taxes: A Revenue-Centered Framework for Explaining Political Order," *The Journal of Conflict Resolution* 49(4): 563–97; and Magaloni, B. (2006), *Voting for Autocracy*, New York: Cambridge University Press.

2

From Fable to Fact

I devote this chapter to the exposition of a fable.[1] While diminutive, it is incisive: It captures the incentives that drive the choices that lead to the failure of states. It is also suggestive, for it points to the conditions under which political order should, or should not, prevail. After expositing this fable, I determine whether it is also informative. It can be so only insofar as the forces that animate its central characters find their parallel in late-century Africa. I devote the last portions of the chapter to arguing that they do and that the story communicated by the fable can therefore bear the weight of the tragedy that befell the continent. The fable can be used – with help – to explore the foundations of political disorder.

---

[1] A rigorous presentation appeared as Bates, R. H., A. Greif, et al. (2002), "Organizing Violence," *The Journal of Conflict Resolution* 46(5): 599–628.

Introduction

A Fable

Consider the following scenario: A community is peopled by a "specialist in violence" and two groups of citizens. Headed by powerful patrons, the groups can act in a unified manner.[2] The specialist in violence earns his living from the use of force; he either seizes the wealth of others or pockets funds they pay for their protection. Sheltered behind their patrons, the citizens generate incomes by engaging in productive labor; but they too can be mobilized either to seize the income of others – or to defend their incomes from seizure. The three personages in this drama repeatedly interact over time. The question is: Can political order prevail in such a setting?

The answer is: Yes. Under certain circumstances, the specialist will chose to use his control of the means of violence to protect rather than to despoil private property. And the groups of citizens will chose to devote their time and energies to labor and leisure and forswear the use of arms, while rewarding the specialist in violence for protecting them against raids by others. In addition, under certain well-specified conditions, these choices will persist in equilibrium, rendering political order a state.

The primary reason for this outcome is that the players interact over time. The specialist in violence and political

---

[2] That is, they have solved the collective action problem.

organizations can therefore condition their future choices on present behavior; that is, they can make threats and inflict punishments and thus shape the behavior of others. Should one group raid or withhold tax payments, the specialist can retaliate by changing from guardian to predator. And should the specialist opportunistically seize the wealth of the member of a group, his defection would trigger punishment by that citizen's confederates: They can withhold tax payments or mobilize for fighting. If not sufficiently paid for the provision of security, the specialist in violence can pay himself: he can turn from guardian to warlord. And if preyed upon or left undefended, then the citizens can furnish their own protection; they can take up arms.

When both the specialist and the citizens turn to punishment, political order breaks down. People become insecure. They also become poor; having to reallocate resources to defense, they have fewer resources to devote to productive activity. The resultant loss of security and prosperity stays the hand of a specialist in violence who might be tempted to engage in predation or of a group that might be tempted to forcefully seize the goods of another or withhold tax payments, thus triggering political disorder.

To better grasp the incentives that animate this story, focus on the choices open to the specialist in violence, as communicated in Figure 2.1. In this figure, the vertical axis represents monetary gains or losses. The further above zero, the

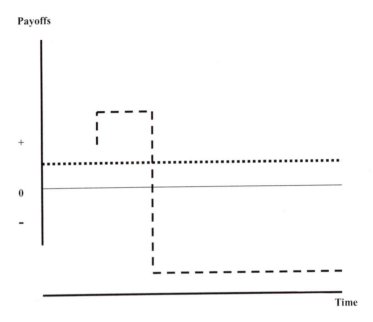

Payoffs on the equilibrium path

....

Payoffs from defection and subsequent punishment

▬ ▬ ▬

Figure 2.1. Payoffs from strategy choices.

greater the payoffs; the further below, the greater the losses. The horizontal axis designates time, with the more immediate payoffs occurring near the origin and the more distant ones further to the right. The dotted line represents the flow of payoffs that result from tax payments; the flow is steady, moderate, and positive in value. The dashed line represents the flow of payoffs that result from predation. Predation yields an immediate benefit: The dashed line leaps above the dotted line, indicating that the income from predation significantly exceeds that from tax payments. But that one period spike then gives way to a stream of losses, as illustrated by the plunge below the zero point that separates gains from losses. Insofar as a decision maker is forward looking, the losses that accrue in the punishment phase caste a shadow over the returns from defection and so temper any wish to engage in predation.

If summed over time, each line – that representing the returns to taxation and that the returns to predation – yields an expected payoff. What would determine their magnitudes? In particular, what would determine whether the value of the variable path, generated by predation, will be more or less attractive than that of the steady path, generated from tax payments? The factors that determine the relative magnitude of these payoffs determine whether the specialist in violence will adhere to the path of play and continue to behave as guardian or veer from that path, engage in predation, and trigger the re-arming of the citizenry and subsequent disorder.

The Conditions of Political Order

One factor is the level of tax revenue. If too low, the benefits of predation may be tempting despite the subsequent costs.[3] A

---

[3] But they may also be if too high. See the discussion in Bates, R. H., A. Greif, et al. (2002), "Organizing Violence."

second is the magnitudes of the rewards that predation might yield. If sufficiently bounteous, the specialist in violence might choose to deviate despite the losses. A third is the specialist's rate of discount. A specialist in violence who is impatient, greedy, or insecure will discount the future payoffs that accrue along the path of play; and she will also discount the penalties that follow an opportunistic deviation. She may therefore find the prospect of predation more attractive than if she were patient, prosperous, or secure.

The fable thus suggests that *the possibility of political order rests on the value of three variables: the level of public revenues, the rewards from predation, and the specialist's rate of discount.* The interplay of these forces helps to determine whether governments safeguard or prey upon the wealth of the land; whether groups of citizens take up arms; and whether there is political order – or state failure.

The tale may be engaging; elsewhere it has been shown to be logically consistent (Bates, Greif et al. 2002). But it is informative only insofar as it captures and incorporates key features of Africa's political landscape. Only insofar as it does so will it offer insight into the tribulations of that continent.

Features of Late-Century Politics

Recall that the scenario was populated by a specialist in violence and by citizens who could, should they choose, take up

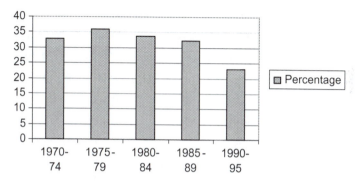

Figure 2.2. Percentage country years in which country ruled by military head of state.

arms. Now note a characteristic feature of late-century politics in Africa: A significant portion of Africa's states were ruled by their military. Turning to Figure 2.2, we find that from the beginning of the 1970s to the end of the 1980s, in more than 30 percent of the observations, Africa's heads of state came from the armed forces.[4] In the 1990s, U.S. president William Clinton and British prime minister Tony Blair heralded the emergence of a "new generation" of African rulers – Yoweri Museveni in Uganda, Paul Kagame in Rwanda, Meles Zenawi in Ethiopia, and Isaias Afwerki in Eritrea – while failing to mention that each had come to power as the head of an armed insurgency. In many states, then, power came from the barrel of a gun (Ottaway 1999).[5]

---

[4] For details of the sample, see Table A.1 in the Appendix.

[5] Lest readers regard the link between coercion and politics to be distinctive of politics in Africa, they might first recall the note sent by the father

Introduction

Not only were heads of states specialists in violence, the citizens, too, frequently took up arms. By way of illustration, consider the case of Chad. At the beginning of our sample period, 1970, Francois Tombalbaya, head of the Parti Progressive Tchadien (PPT), was president of Chad. Tombalbaya belonged to the Sara, an agriculturalist people in the southern portions of the country; the eastern and northern portions were populated by pastoralist peoples. As Tombalbaya consolidated his rule, he posted administrators from the south to govern these other regions. There they imposed policies designed to propagate Sara culture and imposed new taxes on cattle. In response, the pastoralists mounted protests, fomented riots, and formed militias: the Front for the Liberation of Chad (FLT) in the east and the Front for National Liberation (FROLINAT) in the north. It was only by calling for military assistance from France that Tombalbaya remained in power.[6]

of Frederick the Great to the young man's tutors: "[I]n the highest measure ... instill in my son a true love of the military ... and impress on him that nothing in the world can give a prince such fame and honor as the sword and that he would be the most despicable creature on earth if he did not revere it and seek glory from it...." (p. 18 of Asprey, R. B. (1986), *Frederick the Great*, New York: Ticknor and Fields). Recall, too, the rueful words of the dying Louis IV: "I have loved war too much." (http://encarta.msm.com).

[6] For accounts, see Buijtenhuijs, R. (1989), Chad, in *Contemporary West African States*, edited by D. B. Cruise O'Brien, J. Dunn, and R. Rathbone, Cambridge, U.K.: Cambridge University Press; May, R. (2003), Internal Dimensions of Warfare in Chad, in *Readings in African Politics*, edited by T. Young, Oxford: James Currey; Lemarchand, R. (1981), "Chad: The Roots of Chaos," *Current History* (December); Nolutshungu,

From Fable to Fact

Whereas the militarization of Chad marks the opening of the sample period, conflict between militias in Congo (Brazzaville) marks its end. In 1992, a southerner, Pascal Lissouba, became president of Congo(B); in the run up to the next presidential election, the strongman and former president, Denis Sassou-Nguesso, declared his candidacy. As political tensions mounted, each politician mobilized a private army: the Cobras, who supported Sassou-Nguesso, and the Zulus, who supported Pascal Lissouba. Kindled in the provincial towns, fighting between these groups erupted in the capital where the mayor, Bernard Kolelas, had organized his own militia, the Njinjas. Combat between these militias lay waste to one of the major cities of French-speaking Africa.[7]

As seen in Figure 2.3, over the course of the sample period 1970–1995, reports of the formation of militias became more common. With increasing frequency, citizens took up arms and states lost their monopoly over the means of violence.

The scenario depicted at the outset of this chapter thus incorporates two major features of the politics of late

S. C. (1996), *Limits of Anarchy*, Charlottesville: University Press of Virginia; and Azam, J.-P. (2007), The Political Geography of Redistribution, Chap. 6 in *The Political Economy of Economic Growth in Africa, 1960–2000: An Analytic Survey*, edited by B. Ndulu, P. Collier, R. H. Bates, and S. O'Connell, Cambridge, U.K.: Cambridge University Press.

[7] One of the best accounts appears in Bazenguissa-Ganga, R. (2003), The Spread of Political Violence in Congo-Brazzaville, in *Readings in African Politics*, edited by T. Young, Oxford: James Currey.

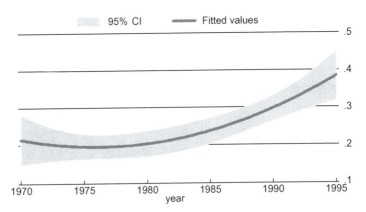

Figure 2.3. Reports of militias by year, percent of observations.

twentieth-century Africa: rule by specialists in violence and the militarization of civic society. In accounting for political disorder, it pointed to three key variables: the level of public revenues received by governments; the magnitude of temptations they face, as determined by the rewards for predation; and the relative weight placed upon them. A moment's reflection leads to the recognition of the possible significance of these variables for the politics of late-century Africa.

Revenues

In the 1970s, a sharp increase in the price of oil triggered global recession. The increased price of energy led to higher costs of production in the advanced industrial economies, resulting in the laying off of labor and a lowering of incomes. For Africa, the result was a decrease in the demand for exports.

In Africa, as in many other developing regions, taxes on trade constitute one of the most important sources of public revenue. As the value of exports from Africa declined, so too did the taxes collected by Africa's governments. In the latter decades of the twentieth century, then, while Africa's people faced a "growth tragedy" (Easterly and Levine 1997), its states faced a crisis of public revenues. The break in the global economy was sharp and unanticipated; and the recovery of public finance required comprehensive and protracted restructuring, involving changes not only in tax rates but also in policies toward trade and industrial development.

The economic forces at play in late-century Africa thus aligned with the conditions in the fable, reducing the revenues of governments. Within the framework of the fable, the decline in public revenues represents a decline in the rewards from public service. In the face of such a reduction, those who control the means of violence find the income derived from the protection of civilians declining relative to the returns from predation. By the logic of the fable, they would therefore be more likely to turn to predation. Rather than providing security, those who controlled the state would become a source of insecurity, as they sought to extract revenue from the wealth of their citizens.

Introduction

Discount Rate

In the fable, if the government becomes more impatient or insecure, the rewards that accrue to those who act as guardians decline in value; so, too, the penalties that would be imposed were they to revert to predation. As the "shadow of the future"[8] thus dissipates, the level of temptation rises: Immediate benefits weigh more heavily than future losses, and incumbents may become more predatory, provoking state failure.

Returning to the empirical record, in the late 1980s, Africa underwent a period of political reform. With the end of the Cold War, the "third wave" of democratization[9] swept across the continent and governments that in the 1980s had been immune to political challenges now faced organized political opponents. As seen in Figure 2.4, whereas from the early 1970s to the mid-1980s, more than *80%* of the country-year observations contained no- or one-party systems, by the mid 1990s, more than 50% experienced multiparty systems. With the shift to multiparty politics, those who presided over Africa's authoritarian governments faced an unanticipated increase in the level of political risk. Few had prepared themselves to compete at the polls; some surely would have chosen

---

[8] The phrase comes from Axelrod, R. (1985), *The Evolution of Cooperation*, New York: Basic Books.

[9] Huntington, S. P. (1991), *The Third Wave*, Norman, OK: Oklahoma University Press.

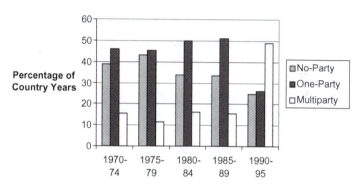

Figure 2.4. Political competition over time.

to govern with more restraint had they known that they might someday be forced from political office and shorn of the protection it afforded. Incumbents became less secure. And by the logic of the fable, they would therefore find the modest rewards that accrue to political guardians less attractive, and the fear of future punishment less daunting, increasing the temptation to engage in predation.

Resources

To a degree that exceeds any other region of the world, the economies of Africa are based on the production of precious minerals, gemstones, petroleum, and other precious commodities. These resources pose a constant temptation to those with military power. Were they to shift from guardian to predator, their future prosperity would nonetheless be ensured, underpinned by the income generated by natural resources.

Introduction

Consider the case of Nigeria, where, in the words of Bill Dudley (1982, p. 92): "[T]he oil boom was a disaster..." – one made worse by military rule. As Dudley states:

> [T]he effect of the oil boom was to convert the military political decision-makers... into a new property-owning, rentier class working in close and direct collaboration with foreign business interests with the sole aim of expropriating the surpluses derived from oil for their private and personal benefit (Dudley 1982, p. 116).

Consider, too, the Sudan or Chad, following the discovery of oil. In both, incumbent regimes turned to repression, the one harrying the Dinka and the other the Sara. Resource wealth thus appears to shape the behavior of elites. In the face of dwindling public resources or insecure political futures, given the availability of wealth from appropriable resources, they could greet with equanimity a future of political disorder. Those immersed in environments richly endowed by nature would therefore be willing to take actions that rendered others insecure, thus triggering state failure.

Conclusion

The logic of the fable highlights the importance of public revenues, democratization, and natural resources and the manner in which they impinge upon the possibility of political order. As we have seen, the elements that affect political order in the fable parallel political forces that shaped the politics of the continent in the later decades of the twentieth century.

While many who have studied Africa have emphasized the political importance of economic collapse, the "resource curse," and the relationship between political competition and political conflict, this account focuses on the logic that systematically links these forces to the political incentives that underlie state failure. Being abstract, the logic is also adaptable; it can play out in a variety of forms. Consider the nature of the groups that may – or may not – transmute into militias. In one setting, they may be the youth wings of political parties; in another, regional coalitions; and in a third, ethnic groups. The same applies to the specialists in violence. In some settings, the military rule; clearly the military specialize in the use of violence. In other instances, it is civilians who govern. Even a civilian head of state presides over police, public prosecutors, and a prison system; by bringing them to bear upon citizens, he too can transform the state into an instrument for predation. In still other instances, the civil service assumes the role of a specialist in violence, using its command of the bureaucracy to redistribute income from the citizens to themselves. Different actors can thus fulfill the major roles in the fable, but their parts are inscribed in a common script. By the choices they make, they animate the sources of political order, induce state failure, thereby enacting the tragedy that engulfed late-century Africa.

Part Two

Sowing the Seeds

3

Political Legacies

B y convention, 1960 marks the year of independence in Africa.[1] Shortly after independence, Africa's new states faced two withering critiques, one mounted by Franz Fanon (1963) and a second by Rene Dumont (1962). Although their indictments overlap, Fanon's targeted their politics whereas Dumont's focused on their policies. In this chapter, I analyze the nature of post-independence politics, emphasizing in particular the nature of political institutions. In Chapter 4, I address the policies chosen by Africa's governments in the post-independence era.

As reported in Chapter 2, by the late 1970s, in more than eighty percent of the country years,[2] opposition parties failed to challenge incumbent heads of state, most often because it was illegal for them to do so (Figure 2.4), and in roughly

---

[1] Of the forty-six states in our sample set of countries, only six had achieved independence prior to 1960; in 1960 alone, fifteen became sovereign.

[2] The sample covers a panel of forty-six countries over twenty years. A single observation therefore constitutes a country year, e.g., Zimbabwe in the year 1970. Thus the origins of this awkward term.

one-third of the country years, military officers served as heads of state (Figure 2.2). The political institutions of post-independence Africa were thus authoritarian. For late-century Africa, the consequence was an increased likelihood of political disorder.

Throughout this chapter, I repeatedly draw illustrations from Zambia's political history. Box 3.1 provides a synopsis, to which the reader may refer while seeking to master the several narratives. Map 3.1 outlines the boundaries of Zambia's provinces, whose political leaders jockeyed for top positions in the ruling party and national government.

The Incumbent's Dilemma

When colonial regimes departed from Africa, they orchestrated their retreat by holding elections and exiting midst the political din. While competitors for office championed the cause of independence and denounced the evils of colonialism, a notable feature of their campaigns was the stress they placed on seizing the "fruits of independence."

In a careful study of the city of Abidjan, Michael Cohen (1974) explores the use of power in Cote d'Ivoire. Rural backers of the ruling party, he noted, used their political connections to move from provincial towns to the national capital (Cohen 1974). Some had been appointed to the boards of state-owned corporations, which produced "palm oil, hardwood,

Political Legacies

Box 3.1. Political highlights, post-independence Zambia

- Zambia achieved independence in 1964, with the UNIP (the United National Independence Party) as the governing party and ANC (the African National Congress) as the opposition.
- High office in the governing party translated into high posts in the government. Kenneth David Kaunda, president of UNIP, became president of Zambia as well, and Reuben Kamanga, a politician from the Eastern Province and vice president of UNIP, served also as vice president of Zambia.
- In 1967, UNIP held internal party elections. A Bemba-speaking bloc captured a majority of the seats in the Central Committee of the ruling party and Simon Kapwepwe, a Bemba-speaker from Northern Province, displaced Reuben Kamanga as vice president.
- In the subsequent general election, Barotse Province (also known as Western Province) joined the Central and Southern provinces in support of ANC.
- In 1969, the president dissolved the quarrelsome Central Committee of UNIP, Eastern Province politicians resumed their posts, and Reuben Kamanga returned as vice president.
- In 1971, the Bemba-speaking politicians, led by Simon Kapwepwe, defected from UNIP, the ruling party, and joined the opposition.

---

rubber . . . and construction equipment" (ibid., pp. 24–5). Others received prized plots of land in the low-density townships, where they built homes, and in the high-density areas, where they constructed new enterprises. As they worked their way up the political hierarchy, Cohen writes, the backers of

Map 3.1. Provinces of Zambia. *Note:* Ndola is the capital of the Copperbelt. *Source:* www.answers.com/topic/ZM-Provinces.png.

the ruling party achieved even more desirable addresses. "[A]dministrative and political control of urban land concessions... turns out to be an extraordinarily sensitive measure of political status within the ruling class," he writes: "Administrative appointments or promotions are often accompanied by approval of an individual's application for land...." (ibid., pp. 44–5). Cohen concludes with a depiction of a housing pyramid, in which the "ministers live in luxurious European-style villas" (p. 47) while their subordinates dwelt in "smaller but very luxurious homes in Cocody," a prosperous suburb (p. 48). To the powerful, he writes, went the rewards: "[T]he winning coalition" used its power to achieve "wealth and position . . . " (p. 6).

Cote d'Ivoire achieved independence in 1960; Zimbabwe, two decades later. As documented by Norma Kriger (2003), freedom fighters, political organizers, and rank-and-file members of Zimbabwe's ruling party began agitating for the rewards of independence. Under intense political pressure from the ruling party, the Ministry of Home Affairs hired 3,500 freedom fighters; the Ministry of Local Government, 2,600 more. The Ministry of Health had to sign on 2,000 and the Central Intelligence Organization more than 1,000 (ibid., p. 178). Once they secured jobs, Kriger writes, the militants agitated for additional benefits: compensation for losses incurred during the struggle for independence, pensions, loans, and land. The political movement that seized the state thus subsequently "built a violent and extractive political order" (ibid., p. 5), as the victors continued to agitate for the fruits of independence.

The pattern has been documented for socialist Zambia (Szeftel 1978) as well as capitalist Nigeria (Schatz 1977). As described by Dumont (1962) and Fanon (1963), independence represented the capture of the state by local political elites who then used power to accumulate wealth.

The ambitions of the elites was equaled by the aspirations of the electorate. Thus Barkan, in his study of elections in

37

post-independence Kenya (1976, 1986); Hayward and Kandeh, in their study of Sierra Leone (1987); and Hayward, when he turned to the study of Ghana (1976), report that constituents viewed politicians as their agents whose job it was to bring material benefits to the local community – jobs, loans, or cash. Those in Kenya, Barkan notes, stoked the fires of political ambition, inciting candidates to bid for political support by contributing funds for the construction of local projects (Barkan 1976). The result, as Allen writes of Benin, was "the exchange of blocs of votes ... for valued goods. ... " (1989, p. 22). Competitive elections came to resemble a political marketplace, in which votes were exchanged for material benefits.

Analysis

In 1983, Gerald Kramer (1983) explored the nature of political competition in a world in which incumbents and challengers compete by distributing material benefits.[3] In his analysis, the voters value private consumption and party labels and the politicians control a fixed stock of material goods. In the competition for votes, the incumbents move first: They distribute benefits in a way designed to return to office, while preserving as large a portion as possible for their own consumption. Once

---

[3] See also Groseclose, T., and J. M. Snyder (1996), "Buying Supermajorities," *American Political Science Review* 90(2): 303–15.

the governing party has proposed its allocation, the opposition then responds with a counteroffer. In this competition, Kramer asks, how will incumbents and challengers behave? How will they play the game?

When seeking to unseat the incumbent and to do so at least expense, Kramer argues, the challenger will bid for the support of those who may be disadvantaged under the incumbent's rule. By offering slightly more than what the incumbent has provided, the challenger can capture their votes and weaken the incumbent's coalition. He can then devote the rest of his resources to obtaining the additional votes necessary to secure a majority. The costs of this strategy will of course be higher the greater the degree to which the voters identify with the party in power.

Anticipating the strategy of the challenger, Kramer argues, the incumbent's best strategy will be to distribute benefits widely. Should he fail to give a segment of the electorate benefits equal to those enjoyed by others, then he simply will have lowered the costs to the challenger of assembling a sufficient number of votes to unseat him.[4] The incumbent will therefore distribute his resources uniformly across all members of the electorate.

---

[4] In addition, if he spends more on one segment of the electorate than upon others, he could lower his own costs – and increase the resources that he could retain for his own consumption – by reducing the differential.

Turning to the voters, Kramer advances the argument an additional step by asking: What if they were to behave strategically? What if they were to back political parties instrumentally, rather than out of an unreasoned sense of loyalty? Behaving strategically, Kramer argues, the voters, in pursuit of private benefits, would reduce their level of party loyalty. The incumbent can purchase the votes of those who strongly identify with the ruling party relatively cheaply; the support of those less loyal would command a higher price. As Kramer demonstrates, when the voters learn to play the system to their advantage they will then extract *all* the benefits on offer. Thus the incumbent's dilemma: Pursuing power to accumulate wealth, they find themselves having to surrender their ill-gotten gains to retain political office.

Did not the history of political competition in Zambia lend support to Kramer's argument, it would be easy to dismiss his analysis as overstylized, abstract, and therefore divorced from the realities of African politics.

The Example of Zambia

When Zambia became independent in 1964, it was governed by UNIP (the United National Independence Party), which had won majorities in all but Central and Southern provinces, where the opposition ANC (the Africa National Congress) held sway. In local council elections, legislative elections,

Political Legacies

bi-elections, and general elections, the governing party relentlessly targeted the opposition's bailiwick. In each round of the elections, it flooded the two provinces with organizers, providing them with housing, running money, and access to petrol from the government's stores. Most relevant for this discussion was the theme of the government's campaigns: "It pays to belong to UNIP." From the government's point of view, those who supported the opposition had merely increased the price of their political loyalty. By refurbishing schools, grading roads, and distributing public monies through local development agencies, the government vigorously bid for votes from the heartland of the opposition.

Naturally, political leaders in other regions deciphered the lesson to be drawn from the government's efforts. Most relevant is the response of those from Luapula, a province long loyal to the governing party. While politicians from the Northern Province dominated the Central Committee and therefore the cabinet as well, the government built a well-surfaced road, a railway, and an oil pipeline through Northern Province to the coast. Political leaders from Luapula Province began to feel that their colleagues from Northern Province were reaping a disproportion of the benefits from holding office. By lowering the level of their loyalty to UNIP, the politicians from Luapula reasoned, they could increase the price of their support for the incumbent regime and secure a larger share of the spoils (Bates 1976). The flirtation of the "Luapulaists" with defection adumbrated later revolts, as other regional blocs listed their grievances and maneuvered to extract benefits from those in power.

From the government's point of view, the costs of retaining office had risen. Threatened with additional provincial defections and thus with the loss of power, the president empanelled a commission to explore the electoral rules; he charged the commission with enquiring into the merits of single-party rule. As documented by Larmer (2006), the commission solemnly convened hearings in each and every region. Having heard testimony in favor and against the abolition of opposition parties, it sensibly performed the task for which it had in fact been convened: It recommended that Zambia become a one-party state.

While the case does not map as clearly onto the matrix of Kramer's model as does that of Zambia, the post-independence politics of Benin suggests similar forces at play. "Resources," Allen writes (1989), "were necessarily limited, but expansion and retention of support implied an ever-increasing pressure for allocation of resources...." (p. 25). The competition for support led to a twenty percent increase in public employment and a forty percent increase in public expenditure – all in the first five years of independence. But then the government encountered a critical constraint: the unwillingness of the central bank, which was controlled by France, to underwrite further increases in spending. By the late 1960s,

Political Legacies

Allen writes, it had become apparent to all that the system based on the competitive supply of "pork" could no longer be sustained (ibid.). The governing elite then put an end to electoral competition.

As in Zambia, in Benin – and elsewhere – incumbents formed single-party regimes. In other instances, and especially under military rulers, the incumbents formed no-party systems. In the single-party regime, the cabinets were dominated by top officials from the ruling party; in the no-party system, the presidents formed cabinets as if picking a personal staff. In either case, in response to the crisis of clientelism, in Allen's phrasing (Allen 1989), or to the high costs of securing wealth from power, in the language of this study, incumbents changed the structure of the political game. They created authoritarian governments.

The New Political Game

Even after the banning of party competition, competitive political forces remained, but they played out within the regime. It was the head of state, rather than the voter, who now became the object of competitive bidding, as minor apparatchiks jockeyed for recognition and competed for political favor and, while doing so, marked down the price of their political loyalty. Political sycophancy replaced constituency service as the best strategy for those with ambitions for office.

Sowing the Seeds

Given the new structure of political competition, it was the supplier rather than the demander of political favors who now held the advantage. In the game of authoritarian politics, the head of state controlled both access to material benefits and control of the means of coercion. And it was to the chief executive that wealth and power now flowed.

In most African states, major financial institutions fell under the control of the chief executive. Allen (1989) notes that presidents in Francophone West Africa kept the ministry of planning in their portfolios, not because they were committed to the formulation of development plans but rather because these ministries received, and disbursed, foreign aid; by controlling them, the president controlled a major source of foreign exchange. In the case of Benin, he noted, the foreign aid channeled through this ministry totaled $600 million in 1980–83 and "thus matched the size of the recurrent budget" (Allen 1989, p. 52). In countries outside of the Francophone zone, the president often controlled the central bank. According to Erwin Blumenthal,[5] the national bank of Zaire maintained such accounts in Brussels, Paris, London, and New York registered in the name of the national president (Blumenthal 1982).

---

[5] Blumenthal had been dispatched by the International Monetary Fund to restructure and manage the finances of Zaire.

Political Legacies

In addition to the financial bureaucracy, the president controlled the means of coercion. Policing remains a national, not a local, activity throughout most of Africa. The office of the president oversaw the ministry of interior. The attorney general, the official prosecutor for the state; the special branch; and the prison system – in most countries, these agencies lodged within the office of the president. In addition, the president controlled special military forces, many organized to suppress internal opposition rather than to defend against external threats. Examples would include Robert Mugabe's Fifth Brigade, which unleashed a reign of terror in opposition areas within five years after independence, or Kwame Nkrumah's President's Own Guard Regiment (POGR), sometimes referred to as his "private army" (Meredith 2005, p. 19). Consider, too, the military units that reported to the president of Zaire. Among them numbered:

A Civil Guard, commanded by his brother-in-law, Kpama Baramoto;

A Special Research and Surveillance Brigade, commanded by General Blaise Bolozi, also related to the President by marriage;

A Special Action Forces, a paramilitary unit, commanded by Honore Ngabanda Nzambo-ku-Atumba, a close aide of Joseph Desire Mobutu and his chief of intelligence;

and a Special Presidential Division, by all accounts the most effective unit of them all, commanded by General Nzimbi Ngabale, also a "close relative" (Nzongola-Ntalaja 2002, p. 154).

With control over wealth and the means of coercion, authoritarian regimes were able to play a game that differed from that played in the era of multiparty politics. As a monopoly supplier of political favors, the president could individually tailor his political offers. Thus Kenneth Kaunda could secure the loyalty of Mainza Chona at lower cost, given the latter's lack of a strong political base, than he could Simon Kapwepe, who enjoyed a large following. Or Joseph Desire Mobutu could recruit Barthelemy Bisegimana to serve as his chief of staff at low cost, given the latter's ambiguous standing as a "citizen" of Rwandan extraction, but had to tolerate the barbs and indulge (some of) the whims of Étienne Tshiesekedi with his strong local backing (Nzongola-Ntalaja 2004). And rather than having to allocate resources in a universalistic and egalitarian manner, the chief executive could employ them to assemble a team of just sufficient political weight for winning. With control over the means of coercion, the president was positioned to make take-it-or-leave-it offers; with control over bounteous benefits and fearsome sanctions, he could prevent efforts by others to collude. The winning coalition would therefore not be egalitarian and universalistic, but rather unequal and minimum winning (Baron and Ferejohn 1989). And by assembling a ruling coalition of small size, the president could divert a larger portion of the "national pie" to his own bank account.

The Shrinking Political Arena

In post-independence Africa, most states became authoritarian (see Figures 2.2 and 2.4): Rather than having to distribute benefits in a universalistic manner, incumbents could now allocate them more narrowly, thereby retaining a greater portion for themselves.

Once thus reconfigured, the political order appeared increasingly to narrow; in the words of Kasfir (1976), in the 1970s, it was "shrinking" in size.[6] In search of resources to consume and to expend in the pursuit of power, elites continued to engage in extraction; their taxes were levied universally. But by channeling benefits to those whom they favored, the elites could offset the costs they inflicted upon those in whose loyalty they sought to invest. The value of the (net) benefits would increase as the number of clients declined, thus generating incentives for the insiders to narrow the definition of what it meant to be loyal.[7] Incentives thus dictated a logic of exclusion.

[6] The phrase is taken from Kasfir, N. (1976), *The Shrinking Political Arena*, Berkeley and Los Angeles: University of California Press.
[7] This analysis draws upon Adam, C. S., and S. A. O'Connell (1999), "Aid, Taxation, and Development in Sub-Saharan Africa," *Economics and*

The criterion for exclusion varied. Politicians often played the nationality card: They thereby sought to exclude foreigners from employment, as in Cote d'Ivoire (Cohen 1974), or from ownership of land, as in Zaire (Lemarchand 2003; Nzongola-Ntalaja 2004). In Zambia and Cote d'Ivoire, they invoked national origins to discredit presidential candidates – Kenneth Kaunda and Alassane Öutarra, respectively – arguing that they had been born to immigrant parents.

Politicians also sought to restrict the benefits provided by government to members of the ruling party. In single-party states, those who were not members could not aspire to public office or to a position in the public portion of the economy. In Sierra Leone, Kpundeh records, clause 139 (3) of the constitution of the ruling party provided that "no one can be appointed or continue to be a permanent secretary 'unless he is a member of the recognized party'" that is, of the All People's Congress (APC), the governing party (Kpundeh 1995, p. 65). So, too, in Zaire: When drafting the 1973 regulations for the service, the civil service commissioner stated "special emphasis, among the conditions required for recruitment, is placed on party militancy and Zairian nationality" (Gould 1980, p. 67). And in Senegal, Boone writes, "licenses were granted to the

Politics 11(3): 225–54; and Bueno de Mesquita, B., A. Smith, et al. (2003), *The Logic of Political Survival*, Cambridge, MA: The MIT Press. See also Kasara, K. (2007), "Tax Me If You Can," *American Political Science Review* 101(1): 159–72.

Political Legacies

bons militants of the UPS [the Senegalese Progressive Union, the ruling political party]" (Boone 1990, as quoted in Tangri 1999, p. 75).

To achieve a deeper familiarity with the meaning of single-party rule, I turn once again to the case of Zambia. After President Kaunda reinstated the Eastern Province politicians to their posts in UNIP's Central Committee (see Box 3.1), several Bemba-speaking leaders defected and formed an opposition party. The government responded by filing trumped-up charges of murder and assault and detained the dissident leaders.

When Simon Kapwepwe, the Bemba-speaking vice president, also defected from UNIP, the government realized that it stood to lose political support in the Luapula, Northern, and Copperbelt provinces – all dominated by Bemba-speakers – and so it could be left in control of fewer than one-half of the provinces in Zambia. The government therefore sought to manipulate the electoral process. Seats in Parliament, it was ruled, belonged to the party, not the person; and when a member crossed the floor, her seat then became vacant, necessitating a bi-election, which it contested vigorously and violently, supporting its candidates with the resources of the state. The government also reverted to repression. When those who defected from the ruling party sought reelection to Parliament, they found their permits for meetings denied, their campaign posters defaced, and their supporters intimidated by gangs of youths and squads of police. In January 1972, one such gang assaulted Simon Kapwepwe. In February, the government banned his party and rounded up and imprisoned more than 100 of its leaders. Many were beaten, some were tortured, and, as already noted, Zambia became a one-party state (Gertzel, Baylies et al. 1984; Larmer 2006).

Following the end of multiparty politics, membership in the ruling party became a form of citizenship. In 1970, the Provincial Conference of UNIP resolved that "the UNIP membership card should be made a legal document for the purpose of identification and holders of the card should be given preferential treatment over non-holders in such spheres as employment, promotions, markets, loans, business, housing and all socio-economic activities" (Larmer 2006, pp. 36–7). Ordinary people could not board public transport, cross bridges or pontoons, or transact in public markets without producing a party card. Those with educations and finances could not hold directorships or posts in state industries, qualify for bursaries or loans, or secure the kinds of positions to which they aspired: ones with a housing allowance, a limousine, and opportunities for travel abroad. By tightly circumscribing the range of potential political beneficiaries, Zambia's political elite more tightly restricted access to economic opportunities.

In some instances, the logic that drove the politics of exclusion appears to have culminated in the formation of a truly

Political Legacies

miniscule elite. In Rwanda, for example, President Juvenel Habyarimana, close family members, and senior members of the family of his wife dominated the financial ministries, the security services, and the ruling party. That the word *akasu*, or small house, came to refer to this group underlines the diminutive size of the inner circle (Prunier 1998). In Kenya, Jomo Kenyatta, his sons, his wives, and their relatives were referred to as the "royal family." Burundi was governed by a small group from Bururi; Zaire by the "Ngbandi" clique from Equateur; and Togo by the Kabye from Kara in the north.

To comprehend the capacity of such small groups to remain in power, it is useful to recall that the security services in Kenya were headed by the president's in-law; that Equateur, Bururi, and Kara provided the military elite in Zaire, Burundi, and Togo, respectively; and that the *akasu* headed a security apparatus that in April 1994 proved capable of killing 800,000 Rwandans.

The restructuring of African political institutions thus triggered a logic of exclusion, resulting in political privilege and economic inequality. Implicit in these transformations lay as well the strengthening of incentives for political elites to deal in private rather than public goods.

Consider a district of 20,000 people, each expecting "his" or "her" politician to provide one dollar in benefits. The creation of one public good, producing a dollar's worth of benefits for each resident, would be likely to cost less than the placing of a dollar in the pocket of each resident. In general, as the number of persons who claim benefits from the political elite rises, the cost advantage to politicians of providing benefits in the form of public rather than private goods increases as well. As Africa's political elite restricted the scope of those entitled to the benefits of independence, this advantage declined. The shrinking of the political arena thus led to a reduction in the incentives for those who sought positions of power to reward their followers with public goods. Private benefits drove out public goods as the coin of the political realm.[8]

Conclusion

In this chapter, I have argued that searching for wealth and power, political elites reconfigured African political institutions, transforming them from multi- to single- or no-party systems or replacing civilian governments with military regimes. They also narrowed the range of those entitled to political benefits. Rather than political independence serving the collective welfare, then, it instead conferred narrowly circumscribed privileges upon those who won out in the competition for political office.

[8] This analysis builds upon Adam, C. S., and S. A. O'Connell (1999), "Aid, Taxation, and Development in Sub-Saharan Africa," *Economics and Politics* 11(3): 225–54; and Bueno de Mesquita, B., A. Smith, et al. (2003), *The Logic of Political Survival*, Cambridge MA: The MIT Press.

Political Legacies

During the struggle for independence, Africa's citizens had embraced politics. In response to the political realities about them, however, in the post-independence era, they increasingly came to view their leaders as a source of insecurity and the state as a source of threat rather than of well-being.

4

Policy Choices

Focusing on the determinants of economic growth in the post-independence period, researchers from the Africa Economic Research Consortium (AERC) isolated a set of "anti-growth" syndromes: styles of policymaking that reduce the rate at which national economies could grow (Ndulu, Collier et al. 2007). Most common is the combination of policies that they designate as "control regimes," which led to:

1. A closed economy.
2. The distortion of key prices in the macroeconomy.
3. The promotion and regulation of industries.
4. The regulation of markets.

In this chapter, I shall describe these policies and discuss their origins and their consequences. Control regimes are economically costly, and I shall explain why incumbents nonetheless retained them, even after their costs were known. The reason, I argue, is that the policies generated political benefits for Africa's authoritarian regimes. They provided elites with sources of income and furnished means for transforming even declining economies into political organizations, enabling politicians to recruit political dependents, willing to fight – if necessary – to keep them in power. While yielding political advantages, however, these policies contributed to the subsequent collapse of Africa's states.

The Content of Control Regimes

As reported by the AERC researchers, governments that adopt control regimes regulate trade, manipulate the interest and exchange rates, and develop close ties with urban-based industries.

The Control of Trade

In the post-independence period, governments imposed tariffs and quantitative controls on a wide range of industrial products. To sell their goods in Africa's markets, foreign firms then had to "jump over" these barriers and to invest in the plant and equipment that would enable them to produce and thus market their goods locally. These policies most frequently targeted the goods most commonly consumed by the residents of poor societies: processed foods, beverages, textiles, shoes, blankets, kerosene, and other consumer products. In at least one case,

Zambia, the government severely restricted the importation of automobiles; and for a brief and inglorious moment, automobiles were produced in Livingstone, a small urban center on the southern border of the country (Elliott 1971).

Macroeconomic Policies

Given the low level of industrialization, investors wishing to establish new firms had to import plant and equipment from abroad. To lower the costs of such investments, governments restructured financial markets. Creating banks that targeted "commerce," "industry," or more broadly "development," they made available loans at low rates of interest to those seeking to invest in projects to which they accorded a high priority. Outside of the Franc zone, they issued their own currencies. Many then employed their control over the banking system to set the rate at which this currency could be exchanged for currencies from abroad. By overvaluing their currency, they set the exchange rate to the advantage of importers: Because they could purchase foreign "dollars" more cheaply, those seeking to invest in local industry could then import plant and equipment at lower cost. Trade barriers having already been set in place, their goods remained protected against foreign competition, whose products would have gained a price advantage as a result of the revaluation of the local currency.

Industrial Regulation

Governments that implemented control regimes also implemented regulatory policies that enhanced the profitability of firms. By licensing, they discouraged entry and protected established producers. When governments themselves owned firms, the governments were certain to prevent new firms from competing with established producers; public enterprises then remained as the monopoly suppliers of their products. Moreover, because governments subsidized the costs of capital, many firms adopted capital-intensive technologies; they then tended to operate most profitably when producing near full capacity. Because the protected markets of Africa were small, the result was the creation of highly concentrated industries, with but one or two large firms in each, with firms operating at low capacity and therefore at high cost. But because the noncompetitive structure of the domestic market conferred on firms the power to set prices, they could remain privately profitable, even while highly inefficient.

The Incidence of Costs and Benefits

When governments artificially increased the value of their currencies, the benefits that they conferred upon the importers of capital equipment were matched by the costs they inflicted on exporters. When foreign dollars converted into fewer cedi (the unit of currency of Ghana), or other African currencies, exporters experienced a reduction in their incomes. In Africa's agrarian economies, most exporters were farmers, who produced coffee, cocoa, sugar, cotton, sisal, and other crops for foreign markets. When governments artificially increased the value of their currencies, they may have protected the profits of industrial firms by imposing tariffs and quantitative restrictions on imports, but they rarely offered similar protection to farmers. Producers of rice in West Africa therefore found themselves competing in local markets with imports from Louisiana, and producers of cassava in Central Africa faced competition from bakers advantaged by the low costs of imported wheat. Trade policies were thus biased against the exporters of cash crops and the producers of food crops as well.

When governments regulated urban industries, they protected the profits of urban firms: By limiting competition, they granted them the power to set prices to their advantage. When governments regulated agriculture, they conferred market power on consumers: They created monopsonies for the purchase of both export and food crops. Governments purchased the cash crops at a low domestic price, sold them at the prices prevailing in international markets, and deposited the difference in the public treasury. They purchased the food crops at prices set to ensure that soldiers, bureaucrats, and urban workers would be assured of low cost food.

In the 1960s, the majority of Africa's population lived in the rural areas and agriculture constituted the largest single industry. The policies thus favored the interests of a minority over those of the vast majority of the population in most states. As noted by Dumont (1966), "In May 1961 a number of farmers north of Brazzaville said to me: 'Independence isn't for us; it's only for the city people'" (p. 17). It was precisely this property of post-independence policies that Dumont condemned.

Control regimes thus benefited the urban and industrial sector; indeed, given the aspiration for industrial development that motivated many policymakers, this was their intent. But they did so at the expense of the great majority of Africa's population – those who lived in the rural areas – and the greatest of Africa's industries – agriculture.

For these policies to persist, opposition to them had to be demobilized. The most likely opponents would be farmers; and because they constituted a political majority, the farmers were dangerous. The political commitment to control regimes could persist, then, only insofar as political challengers lacked an incentive to pursue electoral majorities. Authoritarian institutions thus underpinned the imposition of control regimes.

The relationship between political institutions and public policies is captured by the data in Figures 4.1 and 4.2.

Policy Choices

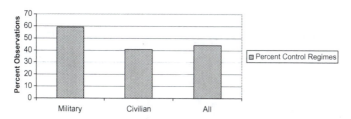

Figure 4.1. Control regimes and military government.

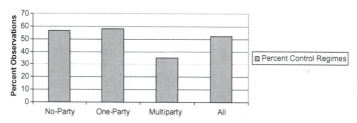

Figure 4.2. Control regimes and party system.

As indicated in Figure 4.1, military governments were far more likely than civilian ones to adopt control regimes. From the period 1970–1995, in more than 50% of the country years, if the data registered the presence of military regimes, they registered the presence of control regimes as well. As shown in Figure 4.2, one- and no-party regimes were also more likely to adopt control regimes, with more than 50% of the observations that centered on no- or single- party systems exhibiting control regimes as well, as compared with but 30% of those with multiparty systems. In this study, I label as authoritarian governments that are headed by soldiers rather than civilians and those civilian regimes that have banned the formation of opposition parties. The data thus suggest an elective affinity between authoritarian politics and interventionist policies in the post-independence period.[1]

Economic Costs and Political Benefits

Given that agriculture is the largest single industry in most African countries, it is not surprising that the economies of countries that imposed control regimes appear to have grown more slowly than others. The AERC research team measured the economic impact of four major "anti-growth" syndromes (Ndulu, Collier et al. 2007). The first was state failure. Next came "inter-temporal redistribution," which most commonly occurred when governments would consume rather than save the proceeds of resource booms. A third was ethnic or regional redistribution, when governments became the political agents of subnational minorities. The fourth was the adoption of control regimes.

Controlling for a variety of factors that might affect growth – the growth rate of trading partners, for example – and

---

[1] See, too, the Appendix. Turn as well to Chapters 4 and 11 of the first volume of Ndulu, B., P. Collier, et al. (2007), *The Political Economy of Economic Growth in Africa, 1960–2000,* 2 vols, Cambridge, U.K.: Cambridge University Press.

correcting for the impact of the growth rate on the choice of policies, the researchers confirmed what most would have expected: that state failure was the most damaging to growth. When states failed in late-century Africa, growth rates fell between 1.8% and 1.9% per annum. More surprising, perhaps, was that they found that the imposition of a control regime led to a loss of roughly 1.6 percentage points per annum in the growth rate, thus rivaling the impact of state failure. State failure was relatively rare, occurring in just more than 10% of the country years, 1970–1995. The imposition of control regimes, however, was most decidedly not: They appear in more than 60% of the country year observations in the late 1970s and early 1980s. The adoption of control regimes thus imposed high costs on Africa's economies.

If the policies harmed the economic interests of most Africans and lowered the growth rate of national economies, then why were they chosen? And, once chosen, why did they remain in place? The answer, I argue, is that the policies served political rather than economic interests.The interventionist style of policymaking enabled governments to target benefits to important constituencies, thus – in the short term, at least – promoting political order. And by transforming industries and markets into political organizations, it enabled governments to spin webs of political obligation and thus forge the political machines that kept them in power.

Sowing the Seeds

Political Benefits

In West Africa, the richer regions lie in the southern portions, which are heavily forested. The Sahelian regions – dry and with uncertain rainfall – have little to offer the international economy[2]; lying inland from the coast, what little they have to offer has necessarily to be shipped at high cost, leaving few profits for producers. Throughout West Africa, then, there exists a disparity between the economies of the coast and interior.

Illustrative is the case of Nigeria. At the time of independence, the economy's most important exports – cocoa, palm oil, and other agricultural products – flowed from the south. Not only did the south have prosperous farmers, but it also was home to the merchants, bankers, and lawyers who provided the services for the export industries. While the north was not rich, it was powerful. It contained more than one-half of Nigeria's population. It was relatively homogeneous: The great majority of its people followed Islam and considered themselves to be Hausa-Fulani. And its emirates provided a means for organizing its people. While relatively poor, then, the region could marshal formidable political forces.

By dint of the north's large size and degree of organization, following independence, its politicians assumed control of the executive branch of the federal government. Pursuing a policy

---

[2] The exception is cotton, which long has faced high tariff barriers in global markets.

Policy Choices

of import substituting industrialization (Helleiner 1966; Little, Scitovsky et al. 1970; Schatz 1977), the government promoted the formation of domestic industries, many of which it convinced to locate in the north. It also placed a disproportion of its development projects in the region. The costs of these initiatives fell largely upon the south, whose consumers paid the higher prices that resulted from tariff protection and whose farmers paid the taxes that financed public investments.

The south's reaction is captured in a statement issued in 1964 by the government of the eastern region:

> Take a look at what they [the North] have done. . . . Kainji Dam Project – about £150 of *our money* when completed – all in the North. . . . Bornu Railway Extension – about £75 million of *our money* when completed – all in the North. . . . Military training and ammunition factories and installations are based in the North, thereby using *your money* to train Northerners to fight Southerners. . . . Building of a road to link the dam site and the Sokoto cement works – £7 million, when completed – all in the North. . . . Total on all these projects about £262 million (italics in original Gboyega 1997, p. 161).

The regional tensions that marked the politics of Nigeria found their parallel elsewhere in Africa. In Togo, General Gnassingbé Eyadéma held power for thirty-eight years; himself from the north, Eyadéma used the powers of the state to extract the wealth of the south for the benefit of his family, the military, and his region. In Ghana and Cote d'Ivoire, it was the

65

south that tended to control the national government; but by choosing northerners for the vice presidency (as in the case of Ghana) or by intervening in the economy and channeling public funds into the interior (as in Cote d'Ivoire), political leaders sought to ease regional tensions.[3]

Turning to East Africa, Uganda, too, was marked by northern poverty and southern prosperity. In Tanzania, the producers of export crops cluster at the higher elevations, where they enjoy bounteous and reliable rainfall and moderate temperatures; the dry climate and arid lands at lower elevations sustain subsistence production. Both Milton Obote in Uganda and Julius Nyerere in Tanzania built their political base in the poorer regions, propounded socialist principles, and imposed control regimes in an effort to redistribute the wealth of the prosperous regions to the semi-arid zones.

While these examples are suggestive, the evidence from Zambia is more compelling. It enables one to observe "in real time," as it were, the process by which regional tensions shaped policy choices. Within a half decade of independence, the United National Independence Party – UNIP, the governing party – was wracked by conflict between regional blocs of

[3] For an analysis of similar tensions in Cameroon, see Bayart, J.-F. (1989), Cameroon, in *Contemporary West African States*, edited by John Dunn, Donal B. Cruise O'Brien, and Richard Rathbone, London: Oxford University Press; and Levine, V. T. (1986), Leadership and Regime Changes in Perspective, in *The Political Economy of Cameroon*, edited by M. G. Schatzberg and I. W. Zartman, New York: Praeger.

politicians, each of whom sought to seize high offices in the ruling party and thus in the government as well. Politicians from the Bemba-speaking districts made up one faction. They came from the Northern and Luapula provinces, and also from Copperbelt Province, the mineral rich region to which Bemba speakers had long migrated in search of employment (see Map 3.1). Another faction consisted of politicians from the Nyanja-speaking provinces: Eastern Province and Lusaka (which includes the city of Lusaka, the national capital). To the side stood the leaders from Barotse, or Western Province, in the southwest; the Central and Southern provinces, largely controlled by the opposition party; and the North-Western Province, which was sparsely inhabited.

At the time of independence, 1964, politicians from the Eastern Province held the vice presidency and the largest single bloc of seats in the Central Committee (see Box 3.1). Three years later, the Bemba-speaking politicians coalesced with those from Central and Southern provinces to seize the vice presidency and capture the Central Committee. The result was a political crisis within the ruling party, as the losers sought to lay claim to the offices they once had held, and to the government posts, with their attendant perquisites, that went with them. In response to this crisis, the president, Kenneth Kaunda, introduced the first of what became known as "economic reforms." In this instance, the reforms involved the takeover of foreign-owned companies. The distribution and management of their assets provided a resource to compensate those who lost out in the competition for power.

In the general elections that followed those within the ruling party, Barotse, whose leaders had allied with the Nyanja-speaking bloc, defected to ANC (the Africa National Congress), thus joining the Central and Southern provinces in the ranks of the opposition. To consolidate support in the six provinces that remained loyal, President Kaunda struck once again, this time nationalizing the copper industry. In 1969, the newly elected vice president of UNIP resigned, sparking rumors of the withdrawal of the Bemba-speaking bloc from the governing party. The president responded with yet another economic "reform," adding the banking and insurance industries to the government's portfolio (see Elliott 1971; Szeftel 1978; Burdette 1988).

In the years following independence, regional conflict thus punctuated the politics of Zambia. In response to the opening of each political fissure, the president extended the scope of the government's control of the economy. By nationalizing firms, gaining control over key sectors, and building a regulatory apparatus about publicly owned firms,[4] the president multiplied the political resources at his command. He posted

---

[4] The firms were known as INDECO (Industrial Development Corporation), FINDECO (Finance and Development Corporation), and MINDECO (Mining Development Corporation), all under ZIMCO (Zambia Industrial and Mining Corporation).

politicians to the boards of each firm in which the government held an interest. And he staffed the bureaucracy that superintended each group of firms with directors chosen from within the ruling party.

Interventionist policies, the example of Zambia suggests, confer upon governments the resources with which to ameliorate political tensions, many arising from conflicts between regions. Control regimes may be expensive, then; they may reduce the rate of economic growth of the national economy. But their costs appear to represent the costs of forging viable political bargains. In Africa, political order is expensive to maintain.

The Maintenance of Authoritarian Regimes

If conflicts between regional political delegations help to account for the adoption of control regimes, the question still remains: Why, once chosen, did they remain in place?

A major reason for the retention of these policies, I would argue, is that they were economically rewarding for those in power – and politically useful as well. They provided the ligaments that bound together Africa's authoritarian regimes.

As we have seen, when imposing control regimes, governments often pegged their currency at a value higher than that which would have been generated by a competitive market. When doing so, they created an excess demand for foreign "dollars." Those in possession of local currency could then purchase foreign currencies at a price that lay below that prevailing in currency markets. Because the demand for foreign exchange exceeded the supply at official prices, the foreign currencies then had to be rationed: Whoever controlled their allocation was now in a position to reward his political followers, his family, and his friends. Control over the central bank creates the opportunity to increase one's wealth and to build a political network.

By appreciating the value of the domestic currency, governments that intervened in currency markets increased the demand for imports. When the currency was set at an artificially high level, those who secured it at the official price could purchase foreign goods more cheaply. By importing those goods and selling them in the domestic market, they could then pocket in local currency the benefit created by the government's manipulation of the exchange rate. But because the currency was set at an artificially high level, those who export earned less in foreign markets: Each dollar earned abroad generated less local income. With the demand for imports increasing and the incentives to export decreasing, governments that set the value of their currency too high soon began to incur trade deficits. To stem these deficits, they began to regulate imports. They blocked the importation of "luxuries" to facilitate the continued importation of "essential" goods, banning the import of liquor, for example, to enable the purchase of medicines or banning the importation of motorcars to safe-guard the purchase of tractors.

Governments that sought to control the value of their money in international markets thus soon found themselves regulating the flow of trade as well. One result was the growth of a bureaucracy to ration access to foreign exchange and the importation of foreign goods. Another was the growth of political machines, as those who controlled and enforced trade regulations conferred the right of access to foreign markets, thereby creating clients: people who owed them their economic fortunes and whose political loyalty they could therefore expect in return.

The intersection of the borders between Rwanda, Uganda, and eastern Zaire (present-day Congo) provides an apt illustration. In 1973, General Juvenal Habyarimana deposed Gregoire Kayibanda as president of Rwanda. Already commander of the armed forces, the new president sought control over the economic bureaucracy as well, including – and perhaps especially – the central bank.

To the west of Rwanda lie some of the most productive lands of Zaire: temperate, well watered, and endowed with rich, volcanic soils. There grows some of the best coffee produced in East Africa. Near the border also lie deposits of gold and some of the last major herds of elephants in Africa. Able to purchase hard currencies at advantageous rates, those upon whom Habyarimana conferred access to foreign exchange at the official rate were at an advantage in the scramble for the riches of eastern Zaire. The president targeted his largesse on his family, his wife's family, and his subordinates in his military, many of whom, like Habyarimana and his wife, came from the northern districts of the country. Funded by members of Rwanda's inner circle, traders and businessmen crossed the border to Zaire and purchased coffee, ivory, and gold. Transporting these goods to the coast, they returned laden with luxuries: liquor, automobiles, appliances, and expensive clothing, to be sold in shops, boutiques, and showrooms owned by friends of the president.[5] Each member of the president's circle then assembled his own political retinue from among those to whom they had extended favors: the granting of foreign exchange, the "right" to market shoes or liquor purchased abroad, or to sell their coffee to private buyers instead of to the state monopoly. The politicians thus cast webs of political obligation about the informal markets to which the government's interventionist policies gave rise.

Recall that the ruling elite controlled not only the economic agencies but also the security services. The political ties that ramified about the regulated economy were forged not only from selective benefits but also from targeted sanctions. Many

---

[5] Meredith, M. (2005), *The State of Africa: A History of Fifty Years of Independence,* London: Free Press. Interviews by the author, Rwanda, 2000.

of the most valuable sources of wealth were illegal: Riches were gleaned in the "shadow economy." Those who secured their income illegally were liable to seizure, prosecution, and detention – or worse, and their vulnerability grew in proportion to their bank accounts. Given that they had violated the law, their prospects – financial and political – lay at the discretion of those who controlled the coercive apparatus of the state.

Conclusion

In this chapter, I have argued that there is an elective affinity between political institutions and policy choices in post-independence Africa. The banning of opposition parties and the end of multiparty politics enabled political elites to adopt and retain economic policies that harmed farmers, even though in many states the rural producers formed a majority of the population. Because politicians competed for the favor of the state house rather than for the backing of citizens, the numerical supremacy of Africa's rural population posed no threat to those in power and so failed to alter their choice of policies.

Because of the incidence of the costs, control regimes effectively constituted a tax on agriculture. If only because agriculture represented the single largest industry in most of Africa's economies, the policies thereby lowered the continent's rate of economic growth. That these policies nonetheless remained in place reflects the political advantages that they conferred: resources that authoritarian elites could employ to ameliorate political tensions, to recruit political clients, and to build political machines, and thereby remain in power.

5

Subnational Tensions

Beneath the political surface of Africa's authoritarian regimes, there were forces at work that sowed the political landscape with multitudinous opportunities for conflict. The economies of Africa's rural communities rendered them politically expansionary, and therefore generated competing claims for land. So long as political order reigned at the national level, and so long as the incumbent regimes could marshal the resources with which to purchase or to compel political restraint, the resultant conflicts could be contained. When states began to fail, however, local conflicts then acquired national significance. They offered opportunities to politicians

---

The argument in this chapter should be viewed as a contribution to the study of Africa's "political geography," as pioneered by Herbst, J. (2000), *States and Power in Africa*, Princeton, NJ: Princeton University Press; Boone, C. (2003), *Political Topographies of the African State: Rural Authority and Institutional Choice*, Cambridge, U.K.: Cambridge University Press; and Azam, J.-P. (2007), The Political Geography of Redistribution, Chapter 6 in *The Political Economy of Economic Growth in Africa, 1960–2000*, edited by B. Ndulu, P. Collier, R. H. Bates, and S. O'Connell, Cambridge, U.K.: Cambridge University Press.

seeking to consolidate political followings, and as national elites were drawn to parochial disputes, Africa's rural citizens, in search of political champions, flocked about them. When political order declined in late-century Africa, it therefore did so precipitously. Competition between local communities thus increased the costs of governing by authoritarian regimes and the pace with which they subsequently collapsed.

Rural Dynamics

To apprehend the forces at play, consider a family and its choice of where to settle.[1] The family will naturally choose to farm the highest-quality land, where its efforts will result in the greatest return. Alternatively, by working such lands, it can secure sufficient food to feed itself at least effort. Now let another family arrive and the population increase. This family must choose between being the second family to settle on the highest-quality land or the first to settle on the land of the next-best quality. Where it settles depends upon the relative magnitude of the output that it can secure in the two locations. For purposes of argument, assume that the differential in land quality is such that this second family, as did the first,

---

[1] This analysis follows Ricardo, D. (1821), *On the Principles of Political Economy and Taxation*, London: John Murray.

secures a higher return to its labor in the highest-quality land. It will then choose to locate adjacent the first family. As the cycle repeats itself over time, a settlement will therefore grow in the lands of higher quality.

A second pattern will also emerge, however: a trickle of settlers to the periphery. Because of diminishing returns, as more families crowd onto the lands of high quality, the increment in production that results from each additional unit of labor declines. New arrivals will therefore eventually find it more attractive to be the first to settle on the lands of lesser quality rather than to be the last to settle on lands of superior quality. There therefore begins a process of dispersal in the settlement pattern.

Arable and Pastoral Production

In Africa, as elsewhere, agriculture involves more than the planting and harvesting of crops. It also involves the breeding and herding of livestock, and this activity too induces the shifting of population to the periphery. When livestock graze, they make extensive use of land. As the core becomes more densely settled, land becomes scarce; it therefore increases in value. To conserve on the use of this resource, farmers therefore tend to shift their livestock to less densely settled areas. In addition, when grazing, cattle, goats, and sheep may wander into the fields, and pastoralism can therefore lower the return from arable production. Farmers therefore seek to separate the two activities, shifting their livestock from the core to the periphery. In the absence of "mixed farming,"[2] the two activities – arable and pastoral production – will be most productive if managed apart.

Investment

Families combine persons of different genders, ages, and generations, and this property furnishes an additional reason for territorial expansion: the opportunity to invest and thereby escape a future dominated by diminishing returns.

As time passes and population increases, without technical change, each additional unit of labor adds less to the total product. If labor is paid its marginal product, then wages fall. Even were the total product to be divided equally, insofar as output increases more slowly than does population, per capita consumption will fall. In either case, the society becomes poorer with the passage of time.

In the face of diminishing returns, out-migration offers an escape from poverty. Because migration is costly, it is likely to

---

[2] This is the change that marked the commercial revolution in European agriculture. See, for example, Timmer, C. P. (1969), "The Turnip, the New Husbandry, and the English Agricultural Revolution," *Quarterly Journal of Economics* 83: 375–96.

be the younger rather than the older generation that migrates, for the younger generation can amortize the costs of migration over a longer stream of earnings. To treat migration as a choice made solely by the younger generation, however, is to fail to recognize other incentives at play. The elders, too, are subject to the consequences of diminishing returns; as population grows, they, too, experience a fall in the wage rate and in average income. As elders, they may be less likely to emigrate. But they, too, would benefit from the out-migration of the young, as their departure would reduce the quantity of labor and therefore raise the earnings of workers in the core. Diminishing returns thus creates an incentive for the elders to invest in the out-migration of the young. The search for an escape from diminishing returns strengthens the incentives to invest in expansion in Africa's rural economies.

Variations in Form

Thus far I have emphasized the economics of territorial expansion. It is important to address the politics as well. In doing so, I draw the conventional distinction between decentralized and centralized societies in Africa (Fortes and Evans-Pritchard 1987). In decentralized societies, politics is dominated by family heads; there is no chief and no bureaucracy. In centralized societies, there exists a chief executive, a retinue of palace officials, and bureaucrats who levy taxes and make war. I note as well a third kind of political system, one in which there is no bureaucracy but the society is spanned by formal institutions called age grades. Despite the variation in the way the societies are structured, each type can be regarded as offering an alternative political solution to a common problem: the need for intergenerational contracts that will promote the peopling of the periphery.

The Family

Migration requires infusions of capital. If a farmer, the junior member will have to be supported until he claims, clears, and cultivates a piece of land. If a pastoralist, he will need to be given stock with which to build a herd. In either case, repayment is deferred. In some instances, the returns to such investments take the form of increased land holdings and a lowering of risk, as the family estate comes to ramify across different ecological zones; in others, it yields a flow of milk, curds, and hides from flocks consigned to the young for safekeeping, or of cattle with which to pay bride price and increase the size and prestige of the lineage. In either case, the elder investors incur costs today; the young recipients later repay; and there arises a flow of resources back to senior members of the family.

The transformation of the family into a means of investment confronts a major dilemma, however. The transactions are separated temporally: The costs fall upon the elders in present time while repayment must of necessity be delayed. In addition, the parties to the transaction are separated by space. The elders cannot monitor the efforts of the young; they cannot assess the validity of excuses for non-repayment, such as the loss of livestock to disease or of crops to grazing wildlife. The potential for opportunism is therefore high, weakening the incentives to invest.

In African societies, the politics of gerontocracy provide one solution to this dilemma. The solution takes the form of the conferral upon the elders of resources and sanctions sufficient to enable them to counter the attractions of defection by the young.

In many African societies, only those who are married and have fathered children of their own can hold seats in political councils, take part in policy debates, and lay claim to prestigious honors. And often it is the elders who control the resources required for the payment of bride wealth. Because of polygamy, they also control a large portion of the stock of marriageable women, and thus the opportunities for the young men to find suitable brides. The elders' control over the possibility of marriage therefore yields them power over the political prospects of the young (see Meillassoux 1981).

If an elder rules that certain rituals have not been properly observed or that certain ceremonies have been improperly performed, then a marriage – or a birth – might not be legitimate. Those whose standing in the family is thus rendered uncertain may therefore lose access to the property or to the political offices controlled by their lineage. That the elders interpret family law therefore places them in a position to govern the allocation of both wealth and power.

Gerontocratic political institutions thus shape the incentives that govern the conduct of the young. Whereas they may prefer to avoid their obligations, given the power of the elders, the young are unlikely to choose to do so. Within a political gerontocracy, the elders control sufficient sanctions to make it in the interests of the young to keep their pledges. Knowing that the young will not defect, the elders are therefore willing to invest; they are willing to sponsor the movement to the frontier. Political structures thus shape economic incentives in ways that strengthen the forces of territorial expansion in rural Africa.[3]

---

[3] See Fortes, M. (1958), Introduction, in *The Developmental Cycle in Domestic Groups*, edited by J. Goody, Cambridge, U.K.: Cambridge University Press; Kenyatta, J. (1953), *Facing Mount Kenya*, London: Secker and Warburg; Sahlins, M. D. (1961), "The Segmentary Lineage: An Organization of Predatory Expansion," *American Anthropologist* 63: 322–45; Sahlins, M. D. (1968), *Tribesmen*, Englewood Cliffs, NJ: Prentice-Hall; Sahlins, M. D. (1971), Tribal Economies, in *Economic Development and Social Change*, edited by G. Dalton, Garden City, NY: Natural History Press for the American Museum of Natural History: 43–61; and Bates, R. H. (1989), *Beyond the Miracle of the Market*, Cambridge, U.K: Cambridge University Press.

Subnational Tensions

Age Grades

In some societies, relationships between generations are explicitly marked by the presence of age grades. In such societies, youths pass through a series of stages before being allowed to marry and assume senior positions in the tribe. Toward the end of their "probationary period," they serve as warriors. One of their tasks is to provide defense; a second is to conquer, seizing cattle and appropriating land. Each age set adds an increment to the total population of the tribe; each is expected to add as well to its productive holdings. As stated by Waller and Sobania, writing of the Masai:

> [T]raditions of nineteenth-century expansion and warfare are structured to link successive stages in their occupation of Maasailand and control of its resources to the progression of age-sets. The advances made by one set are consolidated and exploited by their successors, land resources of stock, grazing and water captured are utilized by elders. In this [process of] ... individual maturation, the continuous flow of age-sets, and community growth and expansion are woven together.... (Waller and Sobania 1994, p. 58).

States

Those who study the origins of political centralization in Africa often stress the role of conflict: The lineages that can conquer

83

or subvert are those that furnish kings (see, for example, Wrigley 1996). They also stress the willingness of followers to obey, that is, to cede power and wealth to the ruling lineage. In search of the factors that shape the level of deference, it is useful to return once again to the role of land, and in particular to the significance of differences in its productivity.

As stressed by Carneiro (1970) and Reyna (1990), when land is of uniform quality, those who feel oppressed can resist simply by exiting. As stressed by Turner (1957), the existence of this option limits the power of headmen and promotes political schism rather than political centralization. When there is a differential in the productivity of the best and next-best lands, however, then political centralization becomes possible. When the high-quality lands are circumscribed by unproductive ones, people will be reluctant to exit, even though coerced or taxed. Thus it is that states formed in the highlands of the Sahara, where the rains fall midst the desert, but rarely in the savannahs, where the uniform productivity of the land made exit a viable strategy (Vansina 1966). Thus, too, the location of states in the richly endowed river valleys, where alluvial soils and abundant moisture promises returns far greater than those in adjacent territories.

Not only do communities in such favored settings tend to be more highly centralized; they also tend to be more densely populated (Stevenson 1968). The price of land is therefore high relative to that of labor. As a result, the monarch can accumulate power. He can do so by exchanging the protection of land rights for political services, such as the payment of taxes or the levying of conscripts.

Like their decentralized counterparts, centralized kingdoms tended to expand. Rather than dispatching youths to settle lands on the periphery, in states, monarchs recruited them into the military and sent them to conquer new territories. The occupation of newly seized territories decreased the pressure of population on the lands of the core; it therefore increased the wage rate in the center. And it brought an influx of wealth from assets captured by the military: taxes from traders and miners, as in Ashanti (Wilks 1975); on ports, as in Dahomey (Polanyi 1991) and Uganda (Wrigley 1996); and on ivory, as in Central Africa (Vansina 1966). By the forceful seizure of resources abroad the military added to the stock of wealth at home. Centralized societies thereby secured higher incomes for their members through expansion and conquest.

Impact on Contemporary Politics

Because of the "imperial peace," traditional states now rarely mobilize for conquest or warfare in Africa; nor, in most cases, do age-grade societies continue to keep their youths under arms. Nonetheless, past conquests by monarchs and warriors created territorial disputes that reverberate to this day and so shape contemporary politics. And even in the present, families organize the out-migration of junior kin, generating conflicts between "strangers" and "sons of the soil." Beneath the surface of national politics there thus lie the political tensions produced by the dynamics of agrarian societies.[4]

Kenya

The Kikuyu of Kenya exemplify the decentralized mode of expansion. In the nineteenth century, the Kikuyu resided on the slopes of Mt. Kenya, where the soils were rich, the temperatures moderate, and where rains fell both in spring and the autumn, enabling the production of two crops a year. As described in detail by Ensminger and Leakey (Leakey 1977), as their numbers rose, families opened up new territory, moving to lower-lying lands at the base of Mt. Kenya. With yet further increases in population, the Kikuyu spread outward. Young people, entrusted with the family herds, were among the first to be dispatched to the frontier; they were soon followed by young couples who planted gardens. Crossing the mountains of Aberdare range, they settled along the upper margins of the escarpment bordering the Rift Valley (Mbithi and Barnes 1975). Doing so, they penetrated into contested terrain: lands grazed by the pastoralists – the Masai to the north and south and the Kalenjin-speakers to the west.

[4] The argument just offered can be viewed as providing "microfoundations" for Fearon's findings regarding the origins of ethnic warps. See Fearon (2004).

Subnational Tensions

In "normal" years, the pastoralists tend to graze on the valley floor; during the dry season, they drive their herds to higher elevations. In periods of drought, they enter forested areas along the rim of the valley, which offers browse that could replace the grasses. For their part, the Kikuyu had found the lands unsettled; when the pastoralists and their herds took refuge in the wooded fringe, the Kikuyu then felt that they had been invaded. By contrast, from the pastoralists' point of view, the Kikuyu had reduced their options for dealing with the risks of nature.

In the 1990s, the conflicts in the Rift Valley moved from the local to the national political agenda. Following violent demonstrations at home and mounting pressures from abroad (Hempstone 1997), President Daniel arap Moi agreed in 1991 to an end to single-party rule. The pastoralists composed the political base of the Kenya African National Union (KANU), the governing party; the Kikuyu steadfastly backed the political opposition. Campaigning for votes in the Rift Valley, opposition politicians backed the cause of the Kikuyu settlers; the incumbents backed the communities whose lands they had "invaded." "Majimboism" – meaning federalism – became a code word for this dispute. Were federalism to be adopted, the more numerous pastoralists would have gained control over the provincial government, leading to the extinguishing of Kikuyu land rights in the Rift Valley – and to ethnic cleansing.

Sowing the Seeds

In the midst of growing insecurity, ambitious elites hurried to build competing political organizations. In the five months that passed from the end of single-party rule to the time of multiparty elections, the Rift Valley became a breeding house for the formation of armed militias, as politicians sought to build reputations for being able to defend rights to land.[5]

Ethiopia

In northwestern Kenya and eastern Uganda, young Karamajong, Pokot, and Samburu, carrying AK-47s rather than spears, pillage the cattle of their neighbors and compel agriculturalists to allow their cattle to graze on their fields (Fratkin, Roth et al. 1994; Jalata 2005). Further north lie the Oromo who, by tradition, initiate a new age set of warriors every eight years.

---

[5] *Daily Nation*, Constituency Review: Laikipia District, July 16, 2002, pp. 11–14; Rutten, M. (2001), "Fresh Killings": The Njoro and Laikipia Violence in the 1997 Kenyan Elections Aftermath, in *Out for the Count: The 1997 General Elections and Prospects for Violence in Kenya*, edited by M. Rutten, A. Mazrui, and F. Gignon, Kampala, Uganda: Fountain Publishers; Mwakikagile, G. (2001), *Ethnic Politics in Kenya and Nigeria*, Huntington, NY: Nova Science Publishers; Kimenyi, M. S., and N. Ndung'u (2005), Sporadic Ethnic Violence: Why Has Kenya Not Experienced a Full Blown Civil War? in *Understanding Civil War: Evidence and Analysis, Volume 1 (Africa)*, edited by P. Collier and N. Sambanis, Washington, DC: The World Bank; *Finance Magazine*, "Kalenjin Liberation Army," September 15, 1992, pp. 20–6; National Council of Churches of Kenya (1992), *The Cursed Arrow*, Nairobi: NCCK; Republic of Kenya, Parliamentary Select Committee (1992), *Report of The Parliamentary Select Committee to Investigate Ethnic Clashes in Western and Other Parts of Kenya*, Nairobi: Kenya Parliament.

Subnational Tensions

Over the centuries, their youthful fighters have helped the Oromo to spread from their homeland in Borena throughout the Ethiopian lowlands, occupying the northeastern territories near the Red Sea and the southwestern regions bordering Kenya.

Until the revolution of 1974, the Ethiopian state rested on foundations forged from traditional states on the highlands. The highland kingdoms embodied the "high culture" of Ethiopia. They defended the elaborate ecclesiastical hierarchy of the Coptic Church, lived off incomes extracted from peasants, and participated in the culture of the imperial court. The Oromo, by contrast, embodied the "low" culture. While a large number are Christian, few Oromo staffed the hierarchy of the church. Their economy is based on pastoralism, not farming, and their society is egalitarian, not hierarchical.

Propelled by the expansionary dynamics of the age-grade system, the Oromo peopled the margins of the Ethiopian state, territorially and ideologically. They became the object of campaigns mounted by the hegemonic center. In the times of the empire, they were forced to convert to Christianity and to tithe to the church; following the revolution, they were forced to surrender their lands to a socialist state. They have been subject to forceful occupation by clients of the national government. In the era of the empire, the center granted court favorites lands on the frontier and the right to enserf the Oromo who occupied them; following the revolution, the central government stationed military units in the periphery and commandeered food and livestock to feed its soldiers and bureaucrats. Seeking economic development, the present government invests in the growing of cotton, sugar, and wheat. More often than not, it locates its projects not in the highly populated center but rather in the less crowded periphery, resulting in the loss of land and water rights for the Oromo (de Waal 1991; Salih and Markakis 1998; Lewis 2001; Marcus 2002).

The politics of Ethiopia is thus marked by conflicts between a dynamic and expansionary society, which has extended its territory and claims to land, and a state system that champions what it regards as the interests of the center. Powerful issues of culture underlie these conflicts. Central, too, are disputes over land.

Uganda

When colonizing East Africa, the British had found it better to work through rather than to displace the kingdom of Buganda.[6] Conferring upon it the status of a protectorate, they employed its administration and police to govern other portions of Uganda. And they rewarded the Baganda for their services by acceding to their territorial claims, which included

---

[6] Uganda is the country, Buganda the territory of the Baganda, one of the tribes that dwell in Uganda. By the same construction, Bunyoro is the kingdom of the Banyoro people.

ownership of several "counties" that Buganda had seized from Bunyoro, a neighboring kingdom. When Milton Obote sought Uganda's independence from Britain, he found it useful to ally with the Baganda, and he allied his UPC (Uganda People's Congress) with the KY (Kabaka Yekka), the court party of the Kabaka, their paramount chief. Implicit in the agreement was his government's support for the land claims of Buganda.

By championing the cause of a party to this dispute, junior politicians could build political ties with a political kingdom, secure a powerful political ally, and thereby accelerate their rise to political prominence. More senior politicians, particularly those within the upper ranks of the UPC, also took advantage of the dispute between the two kingdoms. By threatening to champion the cause of the Bunyoro, they could threaten to alienate the KY, thus destabilizing the Obote regime. In this manner, they sought to extort favors from the central government. The conflict between two of the most powerful states in Uganda thus destabilized the Obote government, driving Uganda close to state failure – and to single-party rule (Kasfir 1976; Kasozi 1994; Hansen and Twaddle 1995; Kabwegyere 1995; Khadiagala 1995).

Conclusion

Africa's peoples, like the rest of us, desire higher incomes. In the absence of technical change, the law of diminishing returns ensures that the growth of population results in immiseration rather than prosperity. To elude the power of that law, people flee to the periphery. In the conditions that prevail in rural Africa, the search for prosperity thus fuels territorial expansion and competing claims to land. In times of political disorder, these local conflicts can accelerate the failure of states.

The dynamics depicted in this chapter are not unique to Africa, of course. They resemble those that shape political conflict in South Asia, although there the protagonists are characterized as "strangers" and "sons of the soil" (Weiner 1978; Brass 1985) rather than as "tribes," as in the literature on Africa. They find their parallel in pre-industrial Europe as well, especially at the time of the migration of the Germans and Goths (Bartlett 1993). That the migrants were known as *jovenes* – or youths – highlights the role that generational succession played in the political dynamics of these societies. The feudal order that emerged in response to these invasions was based on the exchange of protection of property for political service (Bloch 1970). That this exchange characterizes political contracts in much of Africa highlights the broader significance of the dynamics discussed in this chapter.

In the chapter that follows, I turn to the outbreak of political disorder in late-century Africa. As adumbrated in the fable of Chapter 2, it was triggered by elite predation – something rendered more likely because of the lowering value of the resources at the elite's command, their rising level of political insecurity,

Subnational Tensions

and the high levels of temptation they faced, given Africa's resource endowments. While triggered at the elite level, political disorder was marked by the rapid spread of insecurity to the local level, as popular movements rapidly formed and their members took up arms. The nature of Africa's societies helps to account for the speed with which political disorder cascaded from the center to the periphery of Africa's states.

Part Three

Things Fall Apart

6

Things Fall Apart

This chapter gathers together the threads of the argument. It highlights the impact of changes in key variables – the level of public revenues and the elite's rate of discount – arguing that sharp, exogenous shocks helped to drive their value into ranges that threatened the underpinnings of political order. That these changes took place in an environment richly endowed by nature meant that the payoffs to the incumbent elites from defection could rapidly become more attractive than those to good governance. In the context of Africa's resource endowments, the value of these variables needed to alter but little before predation became more attractive than stewardship, thus leading to choices that triggered state failure.

The changes in the values of these variables resulted in part from the impact of previous choices: the forging of

The title purposely echoes Achebe, C. (1975), *Things Fall Apart*, New York: Fawcett Crest.

authoritarian political institutions and the choice of control regimes. It also resulted from sharp external shocks, the first economic recession, resulting from the rise of energy prices, and the second political, resulting from the geo-political realignment that followed the end of the Cold War.

The Decline of Public Revenues

In late-century Africa, governments faced a decline in public revenues, resulting from past policy choices, changes in the global economy, and the predatory behavior of political elites.

The Untaxed Economy

Emizet (1998) notes the web of regulations and controls that Zaire (present-day Congo) imposed upon the producers of primary products. "The goal of these institutional arrangements was to expropriate economic surplus . . . ," he writes (Emizet 1998, p. 105). But, he notes,

> Citizens . . . reacted to the existing institutional arrangements by exiting the official economy, especially in coffee growing and gold regions of Kivu, Upper Congo (*Haut Congo*) and Lower Congo (*Bas Congo*), as well as in the diamond regions of Eastern Kasai (*Kasai Oriental*). . . . The central bank reported that these activities in the second half of the 1970s cost the government an annual average of 15 percent equivalent in tax revenues. (Emizet 1998, pp. 105–6)

In 1982 Zaire had exported 2,000 kg of gold to Belgium; neighboring Burundi had exported less than 1,000. By 1990, it was Zaire that exported less than 1,000 kg of gold to Belgium and Burundi that exported 2,000. Evidence from the diamond industry also suggests high levels of smuggling, with the amount exported illegally being "50 to 100 percent of recorded exports" (Emizet 1998, p. 122). The regulation and taxation of economic activity thus led to the flight of the real economy from the reach of the government.

The Global Economy

In response to sharp increases in energy prices and the costs of capital, in the early 1980s, the level of unemployment in the advanced industrial (OECD; Organisation for Economic Co-operation and Development) nations rose by 50% and the rate of economic growth fell to less than 1%. The demand for imports therefore plummeted and the value of Africa's exports declined. So too, did the revenues generated by taxes on trade, the single largest source of public revenues for most of Africa's governments (see Figure 6.1).

As producers of oil, several African states in fact gained from the rise in petroleum prices; producers of coffee and cocoa also benefited from a late-century price rise, resulting from a sharp drop in exports from Latin America. The governments of the nations that thus prospered launched new

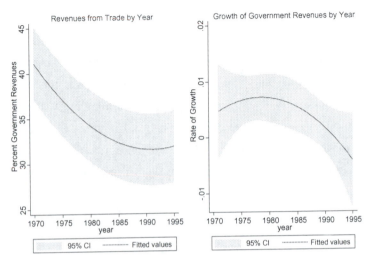

Figure 6.1. Government revenues.

projects, but following the later return of petroleum prices to normal levels, they then found themselves burdened by the costs of these ventures. Many then borrowed, finding willing lenders among banks now flush with deposits from the oil-producing states. When the commodity booms receded, these governments were then faced with the costs of servicing their debts. As had the governments of nations whose export earnings had declined, governments in nations that initially benefited from changes in the global economy therefore found themselves financially strapped.

The late twentieth century marked a time of fiscal crisis for the state in Africa.

Things Fall Apart

Predation

As stated by Sahr John Kpundeh (1995, p. 24), "during the period 1983–1986, it was difficult to distinguish the Sierra Leone government from a private enterprise. . . . " Resisting any attempt to form an independent central bank, Siaka Stevens, its president, pegged the national currency at an artificially high level and began rationing access to it. He allocated a major portion to the National Trading Company, to which he assigned the exclusive rights to import of nearly 100 commodities. As joint owner of the company, Stevens shared in its monopoly profits. Had foreign exchange been allocated by the market rather than by discretion, its sale would have swelled the coffers of the state rather than the bank account of its president.[1]

Even more dramatic was Stevens's plundering of the diamond industry (Reno 1995). Sierra Leone's diamond deposits lay in a region that supported the Sierra Leone People's Party (SLPP), the political opposition, and were worked by a private corporation, the Sierra Leone Selection Trust. As a member of De Beers, the international diamond cartel, Selection Trust tightly regulated diamond production so as to underpin prices

---

[1] See also Reno, W. (1995), *Corruption and State Politics in Sierra Leone*, Cambridge, U.K.: Cambridge University Press; and Reno, W. (2003), Sierra Leone: Warfare in a Post-State Society, in *State Failure and State Weakness in a Time of Terror*, edited by R. I. Rotberg, Cambridge, MA, and Washington, DC: The World Peace Foundation/Brookings Institution: 71–100.

in the global market. The taxes it paid constituted a major portion of the public revenues of Sierra Leone.

Siaka Stevens reconstituted Selection Trust as the National Diamond Mining Company, however. Ostensibly representing the nationalization of the industry, the restructuring instead represented its privatization: Stevens and his cronies dominated both the board and management. By dismantling the controls imposed by Selection Trust, Stevens permitted the working of the alluvial deposits by private individuals, taking care to allocate licenses to political loyalists. Those who entered diamond production formed political colonies in the heartland of the opposition. Serving as local units of the ruling party, they helped to convert – or to intimidate – those about them into supporting the government in power.

Stevens thus benefited financially and politically from the transformation of the diamond industry; the state lost out. Indicative of the magnitude of the diversion of funds is the magnitude of the decline of reported diamond production, which fell from 595,000 carats in 1980 to 48,000 in 1988 (Smillee, Giberie et al. 2000). Also indicative is the decline in tax payments, which fell from $200 million in 1968 to $100 million in 1987 (Musah 2000).

As indicated in Figure 6.2, the share of central government revenues in Sierra Leone's gross domestic product eroded, falling to less than 5% at one point in the 1990s.

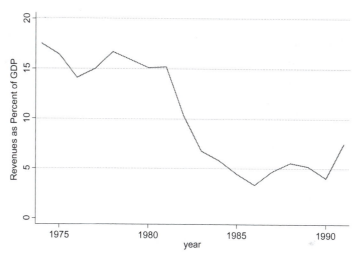

Figure 6.2. Fall of government revenues, Sierra Leone.

The Impact of Declining Revenues

The decline in public revenues adversely impacted the incomes of public employees. Returning once again to Sierra Leone, Sahr Kpundeh provides a vivid example. Interviewing the Freetown Commissioner of Taxes in the md-1980s, he "was shown his pay stub.... If he buys a bag of rice...to feed his family [or] pays...for transportation to and from work every day, his expenses exceed his earnings" (Kpundeh 1995, p. 67). The commissioner therefore worked fewer hours in his public office and more in the private economy. Janet Mac-Gaffey reports similar findings for Kinshasa in 1986. Employees simply could not survive on the salaries paid them by the government, she concludes (MacGaffey 1991).

Given the erosion of public sector salaries, the quality of public services declined. Teachers abandoned their classrooms, nurses left clinics untended, and offices stood empty while public servants turned to private trade in search of income. In addition, the level of corruption rose. In economies in which the government regulated prices, goods disappeared from the shelves; those in charge would sell the product to those willing to pay the market as opposed to the official price. The same was true in post offices, where stamps might be scarce at the window but be available on the street; or in medical or veterinary offices, where pharmaceuticals might be in short supply but available in private clinics. In schools, children found themselves paying for supplies that once were freely provided; in hospitals, patients found it necessary to "tip" to secure a towel, a washcloth, or a bed pan.

A bureaucracy that had been created to facilitate the lives of the citizens began instead to undermine their welfare. Its members began to feed themselves by consuming the time and money of those they once had served.

The most visible of those endowed with the power to coerce was, of course, the military. Their salaries, too, eroded or fell into arrears. Their uniforms became tattered, the quality of food declined in their mess halls, and their equipment malfunctioned and, for want of funds, could not be repaired. In his account of the events leading up to the attempted coup in Kenya in 1982, James Dianga (2002) stresses the lack of such basics as proper clothing, palatable food, and affordable housing. The soldier "has signed a contract with the State," he argues (p. 48). The soldier will defend the state; the state will ensure a decent life for the soldier. But with the "decline in the supply of uniforms," Dianga writes, soldiers began "to wonder why the contract was not being honored" (Dianga 2002, p. 49).

As the value of their salaries declined, soldiers began to pay themselves. Like doctors and nursing aides, they sold services to which the citizens were formally entitled. Most commonly, they regulated access to public thoroughfares. As Kasozi states for Uganda in the mid-1980s:

> Any soldier who needed money ... would just pick an isolated, strategic part of the road, put logs or chains across it, and wait for unfortunate travellers. These twentieth-century highwaymen would rob everyone of anything they fancied: cash, watches, casette radios, clothes, and the like. (Kasozi 1994, p. 152)

In Zaire, soldiers turned to looting. In the early 1990s, Mobutu attempted to draw Étienne Tshisekedi, the leader of the opposition, into his ruling clique. Tshisekedi sought not only an illustrious title – that of prime minister – but also power

Things Fall Apart

and therefore demanded control over the military and the central bank. Mobutu conceded to Tshisekedi's demands, but he pressured him to direct the bank to pay off long-standing debts: arrears built up with utility companies, bills submitted by suppliers of petroleum, transport services, and government stores, and salaries owed civil servants and soldiers. When Tshisekedi refused, Mobutu fired him and then ordered the central bank to pay. The result was a flood of emissions. Soldiers received their salaries in the form of new banknotes; but local merchants, knowing the government to be bankrupt, refused to accept them. Having been paid in scrip deemed to be worthless, the armed forces responded by going on "looting sprees" (Lemarchand 2003), p. 40.[2] They demolished downtown Kinshasa, the national capital, cordoning off commercial blocks, chasing shopkeepers from their premises, smashing windows, and carting off food, clothing, furniture, and appliances. Similar disturbances broke out in Lubumbashi in 1991; in Mbanzu-Ngungu, Goma, and Mbandika in 1992; and in Kisangani, Goma, and Rutshuru in 1993. On the one hand, these "pillages," as they were called, signaled the paucity of the resources with which to pay public servants; on the other they heralded the breakdown of the state.

---

[2] See also Pech, K. (2000), The Hand of War: Mercenaries in the Former Zaire 1996–97, in *Mercenaries: An African Security Dilemma*, edited by A.-F. Musah and J. K. Fayemi, London: Pluto Press; and Nzongola-Ntanlaja, G. (2002), *The Congo from Leopold to Kabila*, London: Zed Books.

Managing Regionalism

The decline of public revenues also made it more difficult to manage regional tensions. In Cote d'Ivoire, for example, political order rested on a series of pacts negotiated between regional elites and the center (see Azam 1994; Boone 2003). Southerners, and in particular the Akan, controlled the center. Prominent in the periphery were the Senoufo, who possessed a well-organized polity in the north. "The complaint of the northerners," Boone writes, was that "their region was impoverished and relegated to backward status in the national political economy.... " (2003, p. 263). To counter mounting discontent, President Houphouët-Boigny launched a series of public initiatives starting projects that led to the opening of parastatal agencies, the construction of roads, and the founding of cotton and livestock industries in the region. Channeling a massive flow of benefits to the area dominated by the Senoufo, the government recruited members of the ruling clans into the agencies that managed these projects (Boone 2003, pp. 267ff).

Should revenues fall, however, the government would be unable to fulfill the periphery's demands. And indeed with the end of the coffee boom of the late 1970s, those in the center could no longer credibly pledge to target the north with largesse (Rapley 1993). The north therefore began to organize against the central government. After the death of Houphouët-Boigny, the forces of the north gathered about Allasane

Öuttara; once prime minister, he now sought to become president. Led by Laurent Gbagbo, southern politicians rallied to check the rise of Öuttara, portraying him as a non-national and therefore ineligible for high office. The courts agreed. Following a coup by soldiers, whom the government had failed to pay, the rival politicians transformed their political organizations into armed militias. Cote d'Ivoire collapsed.[3]

When public revenues begin to decline, then, the likelihood of political disorder increases. When poorly reimbursed, public servants use political power to raise their own pay; they become more predatory. Fiscal dearth also renders it more difficult to induce those who are dissatisfied to continue to participate in the political game, rather than withdraw from it; regional tensions therefore rise, and with them, threats to the integrity of the state. As a result, political order is threatened by the conduct of the elite in the core and of politicians in the periphery of Africa's states.

Political Reform

The decline of public revenues not only triggered efforts by public employees to pay themselves, it also incited popular opposition to those in power. In response to the declining

---

[3] For an incisive analysis, see Azam, J.-P. (2001), "The Redistributive State and Conflicts in Africa," *The Journal of Peace Research* 38(4): 429–44.

quality of public services – and public life – in Africa, people demanded political reform. Citizens called for changes in the institutions that structured political life. They sought to render government the servant of the citizen, rather than her master, and viewed the introduction of multiparty politics and competitive elections as the way of achieving that end. While the impulse for reform originated within Africa itself, it also arose among the continent's creditors, as those who held its debt sought ways to alter the policy choices of its regimes. By rendering governments accountable to their people, they sought to create incentives for them to choose policies that would promote the growth of Africa's economies and bring greater prosperity to its people.

While the reforms were designed to secure political accountability and economic prosperity, they also contributed to political disorder. By raising the level of insecurity for those in power, they strengthened the incentives for them to defect, engaging in predation and thus provoking their citizens to take up arms.

The Local Impulse

Oquaye (1980), writing about life in Ghana, recalls blackouts because of the "breakdown of... electricity supply" (p. 38). Children, he writes, had to drink "from filthying pools" ... and "septic tanks remained un-flushed," raising the risk of disease (ibid., p. 38). Shortages of petrol led to the breakdown of the transport system, resulting in increased prices for food (ibid.). Life in Sierra Leone traced a similar trajectory, as roads and railways in the interior fell into disrepair (Richards 1995); publicly owned companies shut down for lack of power and maintenance (ibid., p. 26). Most galling, Richards reports, was the decline of the educational system, which deprived youths of what their families had regarded as their "birthright" (ibid., p. 177): the chance to acquire skills, to improve their future prospects, and to enhance the quality of their lives. Again and again students rallied in protest against the low quality of their schools. In some instances, their parents joined in these demonstrations. And in reaction, the government dispatched troops to beat, arrest, and detain those taking part (ibid., pp. 54ff).

Growing dissatisfaction with the quality of public services – and punitive response to calls for their improvement – generated calls for political reform. Benin provides an apt illustration. In 1975, the ruling party had endorsed "Marxist-Leninism" and the government had expanded the range of its services and the size of its civil service accordingly. By the late 1980s, however, the government lacked the resources to pay its workers. The result was wave after wave of demonstrations by government employees and increased indiscipline amongst soldiers. While unable to meet the salaries of those it employed, the political elites did manage to find ways to pay itself: In 1988, the issuance of $500 million in unsecured loans to the president and his cronies led to the collapse of three state-owned banks. Such acts inspired further demonstrations, encouraged and cheered on by ambitious challengers to the incumbent regime.

Paralyzed by the mounting waves of protest, the president of Benin, Mathieu Kerekou called for a *"Conference Nationale des Forces Vives...* at which business, professional, religious, labor, and political groups, together with the government, would be given an opportunity to draw up a new constitutional framework" (Meredith 2005, p. 388).[4] Kerekou had expected to dominate the proceedings of the conference, but he failed to do so. Declaring themselves a sovereign assembly, the conferees dissolved the government, appointed a new prime minister, and laid down a schedule for new elections – elections that Kerekou lost to Nicephone Soglo, the assembly's preferred candidate.

An intriguing feature of the reform movement in Africa was the tendency for events in one country to respond to, or to trigger, events in another. Benin's national conference opened February 19, 1990; February 25, a second opened in Congo.

---

[4] See also Heilbrunn, J. (1993), "Social Origins of National Conferences in Benin and Togo," *Journal of Modern African Studies* 31(2): 227–99.

Table 6.1. The spread of political reform

Country	Conference Date	Duration	Election Month	Election Free and Fair	Outcome: Incumbent Ousted	Outcome: Incumbent Retained
Benin	Feb-90	1 week	Feb-91	yes	✓	
			Mar-96	yes	✓	
Congo	Feb-91	3 months	Aug-92	yes	✓	
Gabon	Mar-90	3 weeks	Dec-93	no		✓
Mali	Jul-91	2 weeks	Apr-92	yes	✓	
Niger	Jul-91	6 weeks	Feb-93	yes	✓	
Burkina Faso	Aug-91	2 months	Dec-91	no		✓
Ghana	Aug-91	7 months	Dec-92	yes		✓
Togo	Aug-91	1 month	Aug-93	no		✓
Zaire	Aug-91	1 year	–	–		
Central African Republic	Oct-91	2 months	Aug-92	yes	✓	
Chad	Jan-93	3 months	Jun-96	no		✓

112

Things Fall Apart

The national conference of Benin closed on February 28, 1990; on March 1, that of Gabon opened (Robinson 1994).

As shown in Table 6.1, following five of the first six national conferences, the incumbent head of state was compelled to leave office. The climax came in Zambia, where the national conference called for multiparty elections. News of Kaunda's defeat in these elections (October 1991) resounded throughout the continent: The forces of political reform had claimed one of Africa's "founding fathers." On the one side, those still in office found reason to revise upward their assessment of the magnitude of the threat posed by those clamoring for political reform. On the other, the reformers took heart, finding reason to redouble their efforts.

External Forces

By the end of the 1970s, the international community was fully aware of Africa's economic plight. Emboldened by the reformist mandate bestowed by its president, Robert Mc-Namara, the World Bank had financed a dazzling array of small-farmer and community-level projects. As recounted in its official history, the World Bank's own evaluations revealed a distressingly low rate of return for its Africa projects: "More than any other task the Bank had undertaken, its engagement with Sub-Saharan Africa sapped the institution's... confidence," it reports (Kapur 1997, p. 720). When seeking reasons for the failure of its projects, the Bank found them in "the policy environment." In its famed "Berg Report,"[5] the Bank documented the tendency of Africa's governments to adopt policies that distorted market prices and undermined economic incentives and so crippled growth and development.

In addition to being a financer of projects, the World Bank then became an advisor to governments. In pursuit of policy change, it drew upon two sources of strength. The first was expertise. Through publications, seminars, and the training of public servants, the Bank sought to expose the economic costs of prevailing policies and to offer alternatives. The second was capital. In any given country at any given time, the Bank would normally finance a multitude of projects, the cancellation of any one of which would go largely un-noticed by the national government. To gain the attention of policymakers, Please (1984) writes, the Bank therefore began to bundle its projects into sectoral programs; more would then be at risk were the Bank to suspend its lending. Sectoral programs soon gave way to country programs and to conditionality, as the Bank sought to strengthen further its leverage over policymakers in debtor nations and to sharpen the incentives for policy reform.

[5] World Bank (1981), *Accelerated Development in Sub-Saharan Africa: An Agenda for Action*, Washington, DC: The World Bank.

Things Fall Apart

As Africa's creditors focused on the behavior of African governments, they struggled with the question: Why would these governments adopt policies that undermined economic prosperity? Over time, a consensus emerged: that the behavior of these governments reflected their lack of political accountability. Not being accountable, governments in Africa could adopt policies that conferred concentrated benefits on the elites while imposing widely distributed costs on others. Increasingly, then, the World Bank focused not only on policy choice but also on political reform.[6]

Among the most active of those championing political reform was Keith Jaycox, vice president of the World Bank. In meeting after meeting, conference after conference, and interview after interview, he called for the introduction of political reforms. As reluctant as he may have been to call openly for the introduction of democratic institutions, he left but little doubt that Africa's creditors would welcome the legalization of opposition parties and the holding of competitive elections for political office.

The economic crisis that alienated Africa's citizens thus impelled Africa's creditors to champion political reform as well. Lending further impetus to the two political currents

---

[6] See, for example, World Bank (1989), *Sub-Saharan Africa: From Crisis to Sustainable Growth*, Washington, DC: The World Bank; and World Bank (1991), *Governance and Development*, Washington, DC: The World Bank.

was a second shock at the global level. With the collapse of the Soviet Union, diplomats and security specialists who during the Cold War had been disinclined to unseat authoritarian regimes no longer had reason to object to efforts of economic technocrats to displace them.[7]

The disintegration of the Soviet Union strengthened the position of those inclined to bully rather than to cajole Africa's governments. By way of illustration, consider the demise of Joseph Desire Mobutu, president of Zaire. In the midst of the Cold War, foreign observers had averted their gaze from Mobutus's depredations, largely because of his support in fighting "communism" in southern Africa. Following the fall of the Soviet Union, the hands of those pushing for political reform in Zaire were no longer stayed by those seeking Mobutu's political services. To receive further financial aid, Mobutu – like other tyrants – had now to reform.

In the 1980s, changes in the international environment thus amplified the impact of local political forces that had been calling for reform, and the grasp of Africa's authoritarians on political power became less secure. Abandoned by foreign patrons and facing increasing threats at home, incumbents had increased reason to fear for their political futures. Their time horizons therefore shortened. In the long run, repression

---

[7] See the discussion in Dunning, T., "Conditioning the Effects of Aid: Cold War Politics, Donor Credibility, and Democracy in Africa," *International Organization* 50(2): 409–23.

might increase the level of political disorder, but incumbents had less reason to place great weight on the long run. That even a founding father like Kenneth Kaunda could be turned out of office wondrously focused their minds.

Elite Responses

In response to the call for multipartyism, wily cynics, like Mobutu, sponsored the formation of political parties, rather than banning their formation. Where plurality voting prevailed, the incumbent could then prevail against a fragmented opposition. Others, like Daniel arap Moi of Kenya, took more sinister measures. The shift from Jomo Kenyatta to arap Moi had entailed a shift from a political base centered in the Central Province to one located in the Rift Valley and from an old guard, largely Kikuyu, to a new guard, largely Kalenjin-speaking. The rise of the reform movement imparted new energy to those who had been marginalized. To counter their attacks on his regime, Moi increasingly made use of the coercive powers at his command. Invoking the Preservation of Public Security Act, he jailed his political opponents. His security services were implicated in the killing of a cleric, who was an outspoken proponent of political reform, and a civil servant, who appears to have been too diligent in his enquiries into corruption. When opposition politicians called for an end to the bullying tactics of Moi and his henchmen, they, too, were arrested, tortured, and detained (Hempstone 1997; Anguka 1998; Nnoli 1998; Mwakikagile 2001; Meredith 2005).

Moi was not the only incumbent to bring the powers of the state to bear upon his challengers. So, too, did Gnassingbé Eyadema, the longtime president of Togo. Inspired by events in neighboring Benin, parliamentarians in Togo had also called for a national assembly; to the surprise of many, they succeeded in stripping the president of many of his powers, transferring them to the office of the prime minister – a figure whom they, as legislators, would install in office. As befits a military man, Eyadema fought back. His artillery shelled the palace of the prime minister; his infantry trampled upon those who took to the streets in protest; his police closed newspapers and jailed professionals, party workers, and priests. Eyadema forcefully repressed those who had challenged him and re-appropriated the powers of the presidency (Heilbrunn 1997).

As intimidating as Moi or Eyadema might have been, neither matched the ferocity of the elites of Burundi or Rwanda. While officially a one-party state, throughout the last decades of the twentieth century, Burundi in the 1980s was ruled by its army, and indeed by a small coterie of officers from the province of Bururi. Pressured by donors abroad and, it would appear, misperceiving his popularity at home, Pierre Buyoya, army major and president, agreed to legalize the formation of opposition political parties and to call for elections.

Things Fall Apart

The Front pour la démocratie du Burundi (FRODEBU) constituted the largest challenge to the incumbent regime. Headed
by Melchior Ndadye, FRODEBU appealed to the majority Hutu
and defeated Buyoya, a Tutsi, in the 1993 elections, winning close to two-thirds of the vote. The elections took place
July 10, 1993; on October 2, 1993, Ndadya was assassinated
and the military, slaying tens of thousands of Hutu, returned
to power (Lemarchand 1993; Ngaruko and Nkurunziza 2000;
Ould-Abdallah 2000).

The slaughter in Burundi resonated ominously with events
in neighboring Rwanda. Rwanda, itself divided between Hutu
and Tutsi, was also ruled by its military, clothed in the guise
of a political party, the Mouvement révolutionnaire national
pour le développement (MRND). But whereas Burundi's political elite was drawn largely from the minority Tutsi, that in
Rwanda came from the Hutu, the ethnic majority. More precisely, it came from the portion of the Hutu who originated
in Ruhengiri, a prefecture in the northwestern portion of the
country. The danger posed by reform in Rwanda, then, was not,
as in Burundi, revolution by those long suppressed; rather, it
was that the Hutu majority would split, with the "moderates"
aligning with the Rwanda Patriotic Front (RPF) – the militarized political movement that championed the interests of the
Tutsi – to dislodge their northern brethren from power. And
indeed, as the process of political reform proceeded, such an

alignment became more likely. In the transition government, negotiated under international auspices in Arusha, both the MRND and the RPF gained eleven seats. Should the RPF draw support from one of the minor parties included within the transitional government – the Liberal, the socialist, or the Christian Democratic parties – it could then form a government. The allocation of posts generated at Arusha thus left the hardliners insecure, and they determined to render any alliance between Tutsi and Hutu infeasible.

In neighboring Burundi, the Tutsi-led military had returned to power by assassinating the leadership of the opposition and slaughtering their Hutu supporters. The incumbent regime in Rwanda broadcast these facts widely and portrayed them as foreshadowing the fate of the Hutu, should the RPF come to power. They also launched massacres of their own. By attacking Tutsi in the name of the Hutu, they rendered improbable the forging of political alliances between the RPF and other political parties and incredible the promises of good faith necessary for their construction. In Rwanda, as in Burundi, attempts to introduce political reform thus triggered vindictive reprisals and incumbents inflicted terror and pain upon their citizens in an effort to forestall the loss of power (Prunier 1998; Jones 1999; Jones 2001). Figure 6.3 suggests the level of co-variation between political reform on the one hand and the militarization of civic society on the other.

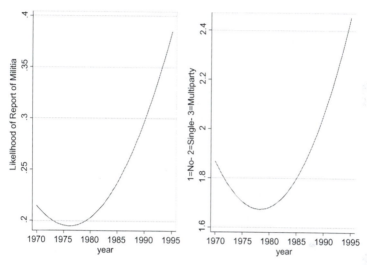

Figure 6.3. Political reform and militarization.

Natural Resources

With the loss of public revenues, governments became more predatory. With the loss of their political monopolies, they became less secure. Recall, once again, the opening fable and the third and last of the variables whose values define the possibility of political order: the level of temptation. Because of their rich endowment of natural resources, many governments in Africa were tempted to abandon their role as guardian and to embrace the role of predator, employing the power of the state to extract wealth from the continent's natural resources.

121

Things Fall Apart

In the midst of economic decline, an alternative source of income lay close at hand: the continent's rich deposits of petroleum, gemstones, and precious metals. To seize such prizes might require the use of force; it might provoke resistance, particularly in the region in which the resources lay. But the short-term benefits would readily outweigh the long-term costs, particularly at a time when governments were finding increasing reason to discount their political futures.

Consider, for example, the Sudan. In 1962, politicians and military from the south rebelled against the central government, protesting its refusal to agree to a federal form of government and its forced incorporation of southern troops into the national army. When Jafar Numeri seized the presidency in 1969, he negotiated an end to the conflict. But in 1978, oil was discovered in a region lying in the south. Numeri then redrew the provincial boundaries of Sudan, effectively placing the oil fields in the portion of the country controlled by the central government. The south's perception of Numeri abruptly changed; once regarded as a guardian of their interests, he now appeared a threat. The south soon took up arms again.[8]

---

[8] See Johnson, D. H. (1995), The Sudan People's Liberation Army and the Problem of Factionalism, in *African Guerillas*, edited by C. Clapham, Oxford, U.K.: James Currey; Johnson, D. H. (2003), *The Root Causes of Sudan's Civil War*, Bloomington, IN: Indiana University Press; and de Waal, A., and A. H. A. Salam (2004), Islamism, State Power, and *Jihad* in Sudan, in *Islamism and its Enemies in the Horn of Africa*, edited by A. de Waal, Bloomington, IN: Indiana University Press.

Consider, too, the case of the Democratic Republic of Congo (previously Zaire). A centralized state under Belgian rule, it fragmented soon after independence. At the forefront of those who sought to dismantle the state was Katanga, a region richly endowed with copper, cobalt, and other minerals. Following Katanga's forceful reintegration into Congo, however, the profits from the mines accrued to the central government – a government presided over by Joseph Desire Mobutu.[9] Succumbing to the temptations offered by these riches, Mobutu became one of the wealthiest men in the world while presiding over the disintegration of Zaire.

For a last example, turn to Angola. In the 1960s, a group of intellectuals, some based in Lisbon and others in Angola's capital city, Luanda, formed the Popular Movement for the

---

[9] See Gould, D. (1980), *Bureaucratic Corruption and Underdevelopment in the Third World: The Case of Zaire*, London: Pergamon Press; Blumenthal, E. (1982), "Zaire: Rapport sur sa Credibilite Financiere Internationale," *La Revue Nouvelle* 77 (November 11): 360–78; MacGaffey, J. (1991), *The Real Economy of Zaire*, Philadelphia: University of Pennsylvania Press; Weiss, H. (1995), Zaire: Collapsed Society, Surviving State, Future Policy, in *Collapsed States*, edited by I. W. Zartman, Boulder, CO: Lynne Rienner; Thom, W. G. (1999), "Congo-Zaire's 1996–1997 Civil War in the Context of Evolving Patterns of Military Conflict in Africa in the Era of Independence," *The Journal of Conflict Studies* 19(2): 93–123; Otunnu, O. (2000), An Historical Analysis of the Invasion of the Rwanda Patriotic Army, in *The Path of a Genocide: The Rwanda Crisis from Uganda to Zaire*, edited by H. Adelman and A. Suhrke, London: Transaction Publishers; and Pech, K. (2000), The Hand of War: Mercenaries in the Former Zaire 1996–97, in *Mercenaries: An African Security Dilemma*, edited by A.-F. Musah and J. K. Fayemi, London: Pluto Press.

Liberation of Angola (MPLA). Part political party, part military force, the MPLA were well positioned when the Portuguese retreated from Africa. Its leaders quickly seized the national capital, the central bureaucracy – and Angola's oil fields. As described by Birmingham (2002), Chabal (2002), and others (Dietrich 2000; Meredith 2005), while the MPLA speaks of serving "the needs of the people," it in fact channels little of Angola's oil wealth to them. The president has retreated to his palace; the party elite to their villas; and their Mercedes and Land Cruisers course through streets of Luanda, which is strewn with garbage and broken glass and inhabited by maimed soldiers.

Other cases could be adduced, each suggesting the manner in which the temptation to defect – that is, to employ the means of violence to engage in predation – can overpower the incentives to employ the means of violence to safeguard life and property. In the midst of fiscal crisis, the temptation increased. So great are the riches offered by Africa's natural resources that, in these instances at least, the rewards to be gained by seizing them appear to have outweighed the prospects of living in the midst of political disorder.

Reverberations

Public revenues declined, political elites became insecure, and the temptation to engage in predation therefore rose in

Africa, amidst abundant opportunities to do so. In the face of increased threats from above, citizens found reason to search for patrons who could help them to safeguard life and property. While inflicting widespread costs, disorder also offered attractive prospects for those willing to invest in the building of political organizations.[10] Among the strategies they could employ, one stood out: the championing of claims to land.

To illustrate the process, we return to the politics of eastern Zaire. During the colonial period, Rwandans settled in the district of Masisi in the northern part of the region, attracted by jobs in the coffee farms and mines of the area. Local chiefs conferred land rights on the aliens in exchange for the payment of tribute. By the 1990s, the Bahunde – the local population – comprised a mere 15% of the population of Masisi and realized that they now constituted a minority, disadvantaged politically by their small numbers and economically by the appropriation

---

[10] This is, of course, a central argument in the work of David Keen. See, for example, Keen, D. (1998), The Economic Functions of Violence in Civil War, *Adelphi Paper 320*, Oxford, U.K.: International Institute for Strategic Studies; Keen, D. (2000), Incentives and Disincentives for Violence, in *Greed and Grievance: Economic Agendas in Civil Wars*, edited by M. Berdal and D. Malone, Boulder, CO: Lynne Rienner; and Keen, D. (2001), The Political Economy of War, in *War and Underdevelopment: The Economic and Social Consequences of Conflict*, Vol. 1, edited by F. Stewart, V. Fitzgerald, and Associates, Oxford, U.K.: Oxford University Press.

of their lands. They therefore began to organize. The Bahunde demanded the dismissal of immigrants from local government offices; some had become chiefs. They demanded a change in the land laws, claiming their rights as "sons of the soil" for the return of properties sold to "strangers." And when Rwanda disintegrated in the east and Zaire beneath them, they took up arms. They grouped their local militias into a loose but armed coalition, called Mayi-Mayi, and backed the fortunes of local politicians who championed the expulsion of the Rwandan immigrants from eastern Zaire (Pech 2000; Mamdani 2001; Nzongola-Ntanlaja 2002; Lemarchand 2003).

Further south in Kivu, the thread that tied the region to Kinshasa, the national capital, had long run through the hands of one Barthelemy Bisengimana, chief of staff for President Joseph Desire Mobutu. Kivu was the home of the Banyamulenge, a group that had migrated from Rwanda and Burundi and taken residence in Zaire. Bisengimana was himself a Tutsi and championed the rights of the Banyamulenge, defending in particular their claims to citizenship and land. But when in the 1980s nationality became a prerequisite for citizenship, Bisengimana became vulnerable. Labeled a Rwandan and therefore a foreigner, he was squeezed out of Mobutu's inner circle. And with the downfall of their advocate in Kinshasa, the Banyamulenge, too, became vulnerable. After the fall of Bisengimana, his enemies – many in search of wealth and power in the frontier territories of eastern Zaire – revoked the citizenship of the Banyamulenge. Because they now could not vote, they could not secure representation on the local councils. Gladly taking their place, others allocated to themselves the perquisites of office: licenses for vehicles, permits for shops, and housing. More important still, given the density of settlement in the region, by labeling the Banyamulenge foreigners, they deprived them of land rights and so themselves gained access to one of the most valuable of resources in Kivu's agrarian economy (Nzongola-Ntanlaja 2002; Lemarchand 2003).

As aliens, the Banyamulenge were thus left exposed to the whims of those with access to power. In response, they took up arms. And when Rwanda invaded Zaire in 1996, their militias joined in the crossing of Zaire, the entry into Kinshasa, the toppling of Mobutu – and the dismembering of the Zairian state.

Conclusion

In late-century Africa, external shocks and forces set in motion by previous decisions led to the erosion of the fiscal foundations of the state. In response to the declining quality of public life, citizens called for political reform, Africa's creditors echoed their demands; and in the early 1990s, both were able to slip the restraints formerly imposed by foreign powers, now less motivated by concerns arising from the Cold War.

Things Fall Apart

In the latter decades of the twentieth century, then, the values of the variables that define the possibility of the state altered. Order gave way to disorder, as elites attacked their own citizens, the latter sought to provide their own security, and states failed in late-century Africa.

7

Conclusion

I n the last decades of the twentieth century, the sinisterly clownish garb of teenage killers in Liberia, the theatrical rage of mobs in Mogadishu, and the dignified suffering of refugees in camps throughout Africa vividly underscored the significance of political order. The power of these images cried out for a response from humanitarians and policymakers. It challenged scholars as well by posing that most innocent and unsettling of questions: Why? Why in late twentieth-century Africa did states fail and things fall apart?

To address these questions, I have retreated to the foundations of my field, which focus on coercion and the properties of the state. I have also re-immersed myself in the politics of Africa. From the first came a theory; from the second, the evidence with which to explore – and to test – its answers.

The realities of contemporary Africa compel us to realize that political order is not a given; it is the product of decisions. There is political order when citizens choose to turn away from military activity and to devote their energies to productive labor and when those who govern – specialists in violence – choose to employ their power to protect rather than to prey upon the wealth that their citizens create. Political order becomes a state when these choices persist as an equilibrium. The foundations of the state lie in the conditions that support that equilibrium; so, too, then, must the origins of state failure.

The fable that framed this analysis highlights the conditions that rendered possible political order. It also suggests the importance of forces unleashed in the late twentieth century. Changes in the global economy and economic mismanagement at home resulted in fiscal dearth: The decline in public revenues led to predation by those in positions of power and to resistance by those whom they ruled. The fall of communism permitted erstwhile patrons to abandon abusive incumbents and enabled those who had protested the quality of governance to lay claim to the rights of political opposition. Loosing support from abroad and facing new threats from within, incumbents faced a sharp and unanticipated increase in the level of political risk. And in many states, the political elite dwelt in the midst of resources bestowed by nature. Those in power could seize control of petroleum deposits or diamond fields and be better off, even though bearing the costs of fighting, than had they continued to subsist on the salaries paid to those who served the public. It was within this ambience of temptation that the value of public finances and the time horizons of elites sharply altered. And it was within the ambience of local tensions, arising from competition over land rights and over the power to allocate them, that political disorder rapidly spread. The conditions that rendered political order an equilibrium no longer prevailed and states collapsed in late-century Africa.

Changing Perspectives

In advancing this argument, I depart in several ways from the current literature on political violence. Rather than focusing on the protest from below – as do Collier and Hoeffler (2004), Fearon and Laitin (2003), Kalyvas (2006), Weinstein (2007), and their predecessors, such as Popkin (1979) and Scott (1976) – I explore its origins "at the top." Rather than probing the motives of rebels or the nature of their organizations, I instead ask: Why would governments adopt policies that impoverish their citizens? Why would they "overextract" wealth from their domains? Why would they alter the distribution of income so grossly that it would become politically unsustainable? By addressing such questions, I explored the ways in which incumbent regimes prepared the field for the forces of political disorder.

Not only do I thus change the point of entry, focusing on the behavior of incumbents rather than insurgents, but I also recast the role of the economic forces. In this work, I did not focus on national income, as do Fearon and Laitin (2003), Collier and Hoeffler (2004), and Sambanis and Hegre (2006)[1]; by the same token, neither did I focus on the impact of poverty, as do the contributors to the World Bank studies of civil war (Collier, Hoeffler et al. 2003). Rather, I traced political disorder to crises in public revenues.

Not only does this work thus depart from contemporary treatments of the role of economic forces. It also offers new perspectives on ethnicity, the resource curse, and democratization, several of the central topics addressed in studies of violence.

Ethnicity

The level of ethnic diversity is greater in the African continent than in other regions of the world.[2] The level of disorder is high. Many therefore hold ethnicity responsible for Africa's political conflicts. To this line of reasoning, I offer two alternatives. The first flows from the inherently expansionary nature of local societies in rural Africa. Because the search for economic well-being underpins a strategy of territorial expansion, groups file competing claims for land rights and political

---

[1] But see Alexander, M. (2007), *Is Poverty to Be Blamed for Civil Wars?* Cambridge MA: Department of Government, Harvard University.

[2] See the regional comparisons offered in Easterly, W., and R. Levine (1997), "Africa's Growth Tragedy: Policies and Ethnic Divisions," *Quarterly Journal of Economics* 112(4): 1203–50.

Conclusion

fissures crisscross the nations of Africa. When states are stable, property rights are secure; when states begin to fail, citizens turn to other sources for their protection. At times of state failure, politicians can therefore marshal political followings and recruit armed militias by championing the defense of land rights. In the midst of state failure, ethnicity may therefore come to the fore. But by this reasoning, it is the product rather than the source of political disorder.

Secondly, given that in most African countries some regions are better endowed than others and that ethnic groups tend to occupy distinct territories, demands for regional redistribution take on an ethnic coloring and regional conflicts assume the guise of ethnic discord. Ethnic conflict is not a "clash of cultures," then, but rather a struggle over the regional allocation of resources.

In discussing ethnicity, I have also noted – and stressed – the disparity between the conclusions drawn from qualitative accounts of political disorder and those drawn from cross-national studies of the relationship between ethnicity and state failure.[3] The first emphasizes the significance of ethnicity; the other, its failure to correlate with measures of political disorder.

---

[3] See also the evidence that the scale of measurement employed in quantitative measures – that is, the use of national averages – fails to capture the variability of interest, which occurs at the subnational level. When such variability is captured in the measurements, then statistical estimates of the relationship between ethnic differences rise. See Murshed and Gates (2003) and Cederman and Girardin (2007).

Rather than arguing for the superiority of a particular method of research, however, I choose instead to combine the two sets of findings. Ethnic tensions do in fact relate to political conflict in Africa, I would argue, but they do so at times of state failure.

The Resource Curse

Just as Africa is the continent most blessed with ethnic diversity, so, too, is it the continent most blessed with natural resource wealth: By one reckoning, 30% of Africa's population live in resource-rich economies, as opposed to 11% elsewhere in the developing world.[4] It is natural, then, that its politics is frequently employed to illustrate the power of the "resource curse": the link between natural resource wealth and political disorder (Collier 2000; Herbst 2000).

Just as observational data for the importance of ethnicity is contradicted by statistical evidence, so, too, do qualitative accounts of the role of precious metals and gemstones contradict the quantitative findings. While Collier and Hoeffler (2004) suggest a close link between the value of primary products and civil wars, their findings have been called into question

---

[4] Collier, P., and S. O'Connell (2007), Opportunities, Choices and Syndromes, Chapter 2 in *The Political Economy of Economic Growth in Africa, 1960–2000*, edited by B. Ndulu, P. Collier, R. H. Bates, and S. O'Connell, Cambridge, U.K.: Cambridge University Press.

Conclusion

by Fearon (2005). They are also called into question by my research, which, like that of Fearon (2005), finds only oil production to be significantly related to the likelihood of political disorder (see Appendix). But just as a combination of the two kinds of evidence generates a deeper understanding of the relationship between ethnicity and conflict, so, too, does it teach us more about the political importance of natural resources.

Qualitative accounts repeatedly link rebel movements to the working of deposits of minerals, gemstones, and other commodities. Statistical investigations largely find little by way of a relationship between natural resource wealth and political violence.[5] The conflicting evidence suggests to me, at least, the importance of the temporal course of political disorder. The first step involves the disintegration of the state; the second, the turmoil that follows. The quantitative evidence bears upon the first; it indicates that states whose economies have been richly endowed are no more likely to fail than are others. The case materials pertain to the subsequent period of disorder. At this stage rival forces seek to seize control over timber, metals,

---

[5] See Fearon, J. D. (2005), "Primary Commodities Exports and Civil War," *Journal of Conflict Resolution* 49(4): 483–507. See also Snyder, R., and R. Bhavani (2005), "Diamonds, Blood and Taxes: A Revenue-Centered Framework for Explaining Political Order," *The Journal of Conflict Resolution* 49(4): 563–597; and Snyder, R. (Forthcoming), "Does Lootable Wealth Breed Disorder? A Political Economy of Extraction Framework," *Comparative Political Studies*.

and gemstones, and to employ the resources that flow from their possession. Resource wealth and political conflict then co-vary.

On the one hand, this revision stands as a critique: Implicitly it charges the earlier literature with having mistaken a symptom of state failure for a cause. On the other, it stands as a positive contribution, suggesting an important feature of the consequences of state failure.

Democratization

In the broader literature on political conflict, scholars treat political reform with caution. New democracies, they find, are politically unstable; far more secure are authoritarian regimes and "consolidated" democracies.[6] By contrast, in the literature on Africa, political reform is widely celebrated and democratization viewed as valuable, both inherently and instrumentally.

---

[6] See Hegre, H., S. Gates, et al. (2001), "Toward a Democratic Civil Peace? Democracy, Political Change and Civil War, 1816–1992," *American Political Science Review* 95(1): 33–48; Hegre, H. (2003), Disentangling Democracy and Development as Determinants of Armed Conflict, paper presented at the annual meeting of the International Studies Association, Portland, Oregon; Goldstone, J., R. Bates, et al. (2005), *A Global Forecasting Model of Political Instability*, McClean, VA: State Failure Task Force, SAIC; Bates, R., D. Epstein, et al. (2006), *Political Instability of Task Force Report, Phase IV Findings*, McLean VA: SAIC; and Epstein, D. L., R. Bates, et al. (2006), "Democratic Transitions," *American Journal of Political Science* 59(3): 551–69.

Conclusion

Clearly, this book can be read as supportive of the arguments of those who are skeptical of the benefits of political
reform. By provoking a sharp, upward revision in the level of
political insecurity of incumbent regimes, I have argued, political reform provoked political disorder. But further reflection
suggests an alternative reading. Recall that it was authoritarianism that lay the foundations for state failure; multiparty
political systems would have been less likely to impose control
regimes as governments that advocated such policies could not
have retained the support of the political majority. Insofar as
authoritarian governments can champion policies that undermine their economies, political reform thus removed a major
source of political instability. Moreover, because the evidence
linking political reform to political disorder derives from less
than a decade of data, it may be misleading. We need further
evidence before we can determine whether the relationship
between political reform and political disorder reported here
represents the turbulence associated with transitional dynamics or constitutes, as the skeptics would have it, the properties
of a new steady state.

State Failure

In the late twentieth century, the political foundations of Africa
were hit with shocks, both economic and political, and subject

to forces that eroded political order. Posed dispassionately, Africa was subject to an experiment, as these forces pushed the value of key variables into ranges in which the possibility of political order became vanishingly small. It was the misfortune of Africa's peoples to be caught in a perfect storm – one in which political fundamentals were so altered that the foundations of the state lay nakedly revealed: a sight that was both horrible – and instructive.

In closing, we return one last time to the fable and turn to a portion that, until now, has remained un-read. The state has collapsed. And in the midst of the disorder that then engulfs the specialist in violence and the citizenry, the government turns to predation while the citizens enlist behind champions who offer protection in exchange for political services. People now dwell in a world wherein the government has turned into a warlord and where they themselves have picked up arms.

Following the logic delineated by Bates, Greif et al. (2002), we can learn more about the subsequent fate of these people. Among the insights we achieve is that in the midst of political disorder, they must trade off between peace and prosperity. When private individuals provide their own protection, one way they can achieve security is by being poor: They can "deter" attacks by having few possessions worth stealing. In the midst of state failure, then, poverty becomes the price of security. Cruelly, the opposite also follows: The price of prosperity is being prepared to fight. In a world in which people provide

Conclusion

their own protection, if they wish to accumulate wealth, they must be prepared to defend it. They must be willing to pick up arms.

Whereas those who live in states can enjoy both security and prosperity, those who live where states have failed must choose whether to be wealthy or secure; without being willing to fight, they cannot be both. The formation of militias midst diamond fields is thus emblematic of the way in which people must live when states fail.

Part Four

Appendix

Cross-National Regressions

T his study has drawn on a combination of argument, narrative, and quantitative data. The narratives form the body of the manuscript and the formal arguments animated the opening fable, but until now the statistical evidence has lurked in the background. It is time for it to step forward.

In this appendix, I first discuss the data and the inferential challenges they posed. I then bring statistical analysis to bear upon the three central phenomena addressed in the study: policy choice, political reform, and political disorder.

The Data

The data form a time series, cross-sectional panel, drawn from 46 countries (see Table A.1) and 26 years (1970–1995).

Most states in Africa achieved independence in the early 1960s, and many initially were unable to gather and report data of key interest to this study. I judged 1970 to offer a suitable

Appendix

Table A.1. Countries in the forty-six-nation sample, 1970–1995

1. Angola	24. Madagascar
2. Benin	25. Malawi
3. Botswana	26. Mali
4. Burkina Faso	27. Mauritania
5. Burundi	28. Mauritius
6. Cameroon	29. Mozambique
7. Cape Verde	30. Namibia
8. Central Africa Republic	31. Niger
9. Chad	32. Nigeria
10. Comoros	33. Rwanda
11. Congo, Republic of	34. São Tomé and Principe
12. Cote d'Ivoire	35. Senegal
13. Djibouti	36. Seychelles
14. Equatorial Guinea	37. Sierra Leone
15. Ethiopia	38. Somalia
16. Gabon	39. Sudan
17. The Gambia	40. Swaziland
18. Ghana	41. Tanzania
19. Guinea	42. Togo
20. Guinea-Bissau	43. Uganda
21. Kenya	44. Dem. Rep. of the Congo
22. Lesotho	45. Zambia
23. Liberia	46. Zimbabwe

compromise between the depth of the panels and the problems posed by missing data, and 1970 therefore became the initial year of the sample. Beginning this project in 1997, I initially adopted 1995 as the terminal year; the data come from

Appendix

published sources and a two-year time lag between the time of writing and the date of the most current observation seemed the best that could be achieved. As no other end date would be any less arbitrary and as attempts at currency would run afoul pauses for analysis and publication, I have therefore stuck with 1995 as the cutoff date for the sample.[1]

The panel is composed of all independent countries in sub-Saharan Africa, with the exception of South Africa. The magnitude of the South African economy and the character of its politics rendered it a major – and potentially highly influential – outlier.

Working with a talented team of graduate students, I gathered economic and financial data from sources commonly employed by those building cross-national samples of country-level data. Tables A.2, A.6, and A.9 describe the characteristics of the measures employed in each portion of the analysis and the sources from which they were taken.

General Overview

Shaping the strategy of estimation were the extent and incidence of missing data, difficulties of measurement, and patterns of dependence among the observations.

---

[1] The data can be found at http://Africa.gov.harvard.edu. Macartan Humphreys built the original Web site; Maria Petrova updated it. As I write, I am continuing to update the data.

Appendix

Missingness

Some countries in some years failed to report statistics. To the extent that the problem originated from the institutional weakness of Africa's newly independent states, limiting the depth of the panel provided a remedy. The problem also arose, however, from the subsequent collapse of some of these states. Because of the potential for selection bias, this source required a more sophisticated response.

Until recently, scholars, when faced with missing data, have reverted to "list-wise deletion": If data for a *variable* were missing, then the *case* was dropped from the data set. Not only does the dropping of cases throw information away and thus render estimates inefficient, but also, should the data not be missing completely at random, then list-wise deletion may render the estimates biased (King, Honeker et al. 2001). For the reasons just discussed, in this instance, the likelihood of bias approaches certitude. Employing the methods championed by Rubin (1996) and implemented by Schafer (1997), I therefore created multiple data sets that incorporate values for missing observations that have been statistically imputed using variables whose values could be observed. I have posted the resultant data sets on my Web site (http://people.iq.harvard.edu/~Rbates/), along with the R-scripts employed to generate them.

Appendix

Qualitative Dependent Variable

Having reviewed the problems confronting those who seek accurate body counts, I simply could not bring myself to use reported deaths as a measure of disorder.[2] I attempted to calculate the percent of a nation's territory controlled by rebels, but accurate estimates of this variable also proved difficult to devise. Data on refugees and displaced persons appeared to be much more precise; but the systematic reporting of these data began late in the sample period and would therefore have necessitated a severe truncation of the panel.

I sought to use the formation of militias as my indicator of state failure. I could not use the number of militias as a dependent variable, however: Given that militias often change their names, I ran the risk of double-counting; and given that some sought to hide their identity, I ran the risk of undercounting. Nor could I make use of the number of combatants; public estimates varied wildly, reflecting the incentives of the rebel side to claim popular backing and of the government to deprecate such claims.

---

[2] For an illuminating discussion of the accuracy of battle death data in the Liberian civil war, see the appendix to Ellis, S. (1999), *The Making of Anarchy*, New York: New York University Press. For more general and technical discussions, see the papers made available through the Households in Conflict Network, which can be accessed on the World Wide Web (www.hicn.org).

Appendix

In the end, I therefore chose to employ a categorical measure. I created an indicator that took on the value of "1" if there was any report[3] of an armed militia in a given country in a given year and a "0" otherwise.

Patterns of Dependence

To correct for the impart of correlation across time periods and within countries on the standard errors, I made use of robust standard errors, clustering by country. The presence of militias at one time might well affect the likelihood of their being reported at another. I therefore adopted the techniques devised by Beck, Katz et al. (1998), introducing cubic splines to correct my estimates for the impact of temporal dependence arising from the events themselves.

Possibilities also arise for interdependence among countries within the cross sections. I introduced "period dummies" to control for the impact of shocks that might be common to the whole sample set of countries: the rise of oil prices in the 1970s, for example, or the end of the Cold War in the late 1980s. For each observation, I also computed[4] the value of the dependent variable in neighboring states, allowing me to control for the possibility, say, that the likelihood of political reform or

---

[3] Reports are from the sources listed in Table A.9.
[4] Computations were conducted with the assistance of James Habyarimana.

Appendix

disorder in a country in a given year was related to the extent of political reform or disorder in its neighbors.

Discussion

Given the nature of the data, the challenge therefore became to draw precise and unbiased estimates from multiple, imputed sets of time series, cross-sectional data, with a binary dependent variable, controlling for the sources of error discussed above. Given the state of the art, the properties of the data set limited my choice of models.

The following three sections present the estimates that I have obtained.[5]

Policy Choices

I attributed the initial choice of control regimes in part to demands for regional redistribution. Their persistence I attributed to the authoritarian nature of governments, which virtually disenfranchised those who bore the costs of these policies. Table A.2 presents the variables employed in the analysis of policy choices. Table A.3 presents estimates from a

---

[5] I was assisted in these labors by Matthew Hindman and Marc Alexander, plus others who labored 'round Gary King's shop at Harvard University, Olivia Lau and Rebecca Nelson in particular. I owe special thanks to Jas Sekhon.

Table A.2. Variables employed in analysis of policy choices

	Measure	Mean	Standard Deviation	Source
Dependent Variable				
Control regime	1 = Yes 0 = No	0.51	0.500	Ndulu, Collier, et al. 2007
Syndrome-free	1 = Yes 0 = No	0.251	0.434	Ndulu, Collier, et al. 2007
Independent Variables				
Authoritarian regime	1 if no- or single-party. 0 otherwise	0.704	0.456	*Keesings Contemporary Archives* *Africa Confidential* *Economist Intelligence Unit*
Military government	1 if head of state is or ever has been military professional. 0 otherwise	0.441	0.497	*Keesings Contemporary Archives* *Africa Confidential* *Economist Intelligence Unit*

Privileged region	1 = yes 0 = No	0.891	0.331	Harvard research team
President from non-privileged region	1 = yes 0 = No	0.570	0.495	Harvard research team
Period1	1 if 1970–74 0 otherwise			
Period2	1 if 1975–79 0 otherwise			
Period3	1 if 1980–84 0 otherwise			
Period4	1 if 1985–89 0 otherwise			

Note: The variables "authoritarian regime?" and "military government?" have been lagged by one year.
Ndulu, B., P. Collier, et al. 2007. *The Political Economy of Economic Growth in Africa, 1960–2000*. 2 vols. Cambridge, U.K.: Cambridge University Press.

Table A.3. Correlates of policy regimes, pooled sample

	Control Regime				Syndrome-Free Policy Choices			
	Coefficient (1)	P > t	Coefficient (2)	P > t	Coefficient (3)	P > t	Coefficient (4)	P > t
Authoritarian regime	0.214 (0.473)	0.636			−0.826 (−1.614)	0.106		
Military government			0.143 (0.287)	0.774			−1.390 (−2.415)	0.016
Privileged region	2.198 (1.746)	0.082	2.207 (1.735)	0.084	−3.530 (−2.877)	0.004	−3.547 (−3.503)	0.000
President from non-privileged region	0.982 (2.191)	0.028	0.971 (2.100)	0.036	−0.329 (−0.596)	0.552	−0.185 (−0.322)	0.748
Period1	1.102 (2.825)	0.005	1.122 (2.817)	0.005	−0.586 (−1.512)	0.131	−0.779 (−1.984)	0.047
Period2	1.609 (5.129)	0.000	1.646 (5.150)	0.000	−1.580 (−3.278)	0.001	−1.819 (−3.907)	0.000
Period3	1.540 (5.048)	0.000	1.573 (5.147)	0.000	−1.796 (−3.614)	0.000	−1.989 (−4.159)	0.000
Period4	1.148 (4.575)	0.000	1.171 (4.650)	0.000	−1.153 (−3.311)	0.001	−1.235 (−3.386)	0.001
Constant	−3.704 (−2.909)	0.004	−3.631 (−2.907)	0.004	3.561 (2.757)	0.006	3.530 (3.526)	0.000
Observations	1150		1150		1150		1150	

Note: t statistics in parentheses. Robust standard errors, grouped by country.

pooled set of data; given the qualitative nature of the dependent variables (see Table A.2), the estimates are based upon a logit model. When, I introduce country-specific fixed effects (Table A.4), I employ a conditional logit model.

The dependent variables are policy choices: the choice of "control regime" in the left-hand panel (equations 1 and 2) and "syndrome-free" policymaking on the right (equations 3 and 4).[6] In both sets of equations, the period dummies (Period 1 . . . Period 4) help to control for time-specific effects, such as changes in the global economy or the international balance of power. The reference category is 1990–95 (Period 5).

In Table A.3, the variable "privileged region" takes the value 1 when there exists major regional inequality in a country and 0 when there does not. Such inequalities can arise because of differences in soil quality (in 53% of the cases in which such inequalities were judged to exist), mineral deposits (in 47% of the cases), or a climate favorable to the production of export crops (in 92% of the cases). As this variable is time invariant, it could not be incorporated into fixed effects equations (Table A.4). I therefore make use instead of a variable that takes on the value 1 if the incumbent president is from a non-privileged region and 0 if not. In Table A.4, the coefficients on

[6] For details concerning the content of these policies, see Chapter 4.

Table A.4. Correlates of policy regimes, conditional logit

	Control Regime				Syndrome-Free Policy Choices			
	Coefficient (1)	P > t	Coefficient (2)	P > t	Coefficient (3)	P > t	Coefficient (4)	P > t
Authoritarian regime	0.434 (1.113)	0.268			−0.081 (−0.209)	0.835		
Military government			0.070 (0.177)	0.859			−0.30791 (−0.652)	0.517
President from non-privileged region	0.823 (1.972)	0.051	2.024 (2.104)	0.037	−1.567 (−2.657)	0.020	−1.5256 (−2.498)	0.029
Period1	2.060 (6.029)	0.000	2.024 (5.873)	0.000	−1.161 (−3.291)	0.001	−1.1956 (−3.287)	0.001
Period2	3.981 (9.153)	0.000	4.047 (9.315)	0.000	−3.609 (−5.411)	0.000	−3.6319 (−5.668)	0.000
Period3	4.300 (9.128)	0.000	4.310 (9.204)	0.000	−4.571 (−3.904)	0.001	−4.5604 (−5.504)	0.001
Period4	2.604 (7.262)	0.000	2.657 (7.406)	0.000	−2.215 (−5.532)	0.000	−2.1527 (−5.504)	0.000
Constant	−3.704 (−2.909)	0.004	−3.631 (−2.907)	0.004				
Observations	700		700		675		675	

Note: t statistics in parentheses.

154

Appendix

the variable therefore indicate the changes in the likelihood of choosing a particular policy regime when a president from a non-privileged region enters office.

"Authoritarianism" takes on the value 1 when no- or single-party systems are in place. The variable "military government" takes on the value of 1 when the head of state is, or was, a professional soldier, and the coefficient indicates the difference in the likelihood of the respective policy being chosen by a military as opposed to civilian regime. In Table A.3, the coefficients therefore indicate the difference in the likelihood of a given policy being chosen when a government is "authoritarian" or military as opposed to when a government is not. In Table A.4, the coefficients indicate the changes in the likelihood of a given policy choice when associated with changes in the type of government.

The estimates in Table A.3 indicate that countries characterized by regional inequality are significantly more likely to adopt control regimes and significantly less likely to adopt "syndrome-free" or market-oriented economic policies. The coefficients on the period dummies confirm that control regimes were abandoned following the end of the Cold War and that syndrome-free policymaking became more common.

In Table A.4, the temporal dummies remain highly significant when country-specific fixed effects are introduced into the estimates. They strongly underscore the impact of "global"

Table A.5. First differences – determinants of policy choice, pooled sample

	Change in Probability of Adopting Control Regime				Change in Probability of Adopting Syndrome-Free Policies			
	(1)		(2)		(3)		(4)	
	Percentage Change in Probability	95% Confidence Interval	Percentage Change in Probability	95% Confidence Interval	Percentage Change in Probability	95% Confidence Interval	Percentage Change in Probability	95% Confidence Interval
Authoritarian regime	0.031	0.009 0.059			-0.067	-0.114 0.034		
Military government			0.023	0.003 0.051			-0.135	-0.212 -0.075
Privileged region	0.233	0.18 0.289	0.254	0.197 0.31	-0.515	-0.581 -0.452	-0.500	-0.574 -0.444
Period1	0.053	0.02 0.095	0.065	0.025 0.112	-0.012	-0.034 -0.009	-0.025	-0.057 -0.003
Period2	0.125	0.069 0.195	0.15	0.09 0.227	-0.100	-0.174 -0.047	-0.132	-0.215 -0.068
Period3	0.138	0.077 0.218	0.159	0.094 0.24	-0.132	-0.225 -0.066	-0.153	-0.254 -0.08
Period4	0.092	0.044 0.154	0.11	0.057 0.174	-0.069	-0.137 -0.022	-0.07	-0.15 -0.03

Note: In each instance, the coefficient indicates the percentage change in probability of the choice of policy regime resulting from a movement from 0 to 1 in the value of the independent variable.

forces on the choice of policy regime. The estimates confirm that when presidents from a non-privileged region assume power, the likelihood of adopting a control regime significantly increases. The coefficients on the type of government (Table A.3) indicate that authoritarian governments and military rgimes are less likely to adopt syndrome-free styles of policymaking.

Table A.5 provides data on the magnitude of the relationships between the independent and dependent variables and is based upon the coefficients in equation 1 of Table A.4. The estimates are produced by varying each variable from 0 to 1 while holding all others at their modal values (in this instance, 0).[7] Countries with a privileged region are roughly 25% more likely to impose a control regime and 50% less likely to lack syndrome-free policies. The late 1970s to early 1980s emerges as the period in which governments were most likely to adopt interventionist policies; countries were roughly 12 to 15% more likely to adopt control regimes and 13 to 15% less likely to adopt market friendly economic measures in the late 1970s and early 1980s by comparison with the 1990s. Authoritarian governments were roughly 3% more likely to adopt control regimes and 7% less likely to adopt syndrome-free policy regimes; military governments, 2% and 14%, respectively.

---

[7] The first two numbers in a given row indicate the lower and upper bounds of the 95% confidence interval of these estimated magnitude of the response of the dependent variable.

Table A.6. Variables pertaining to political reform

	Measure	Mean	Standard Deviation	Source
Dependent Variable				
Multiparty system	1 = Yes 0 = No- or single-party	0.208	0.406	Data collected by research team from *Keesings Contemporary Archives* *Africa Confidential*
Reform	1 = Yes: Civilian government 0 = Professional soldier head of state	0.637	0.481	*Economist Intelligence Unit*
Independent Variables				
Income	Log of GDP per capita (PPP)	1173.38	974.723	*Penn World Tables Mark 5.6*
Urban population	Percent of population living	25.849	13.476	*World Development Indicators*
Literacy	Percent of adult population that is illiterate	58.917	19.921	*World Development Indicators*
Modernization	Factor score derived from principal components analysis of INCOME, LITERACY, and URBAN POPULATION	−0.018	0.022	
Petroleum	Value of exports per capita in constant U.S. dollars ('000)	87.010	14.331	Data collected by research team from commercial sources

Variable	Description			Source
Trade taxes	Percentage central government revenues from taxes on trade	34.23	0.659	*World Development Indicators*
Business cycle	Weighted average growth rate of G7 economies	0.021	0.019	Data created by research team using data from *Penn World Tables Mark 5.6*
Aid dependence	Foreign aid percent of central government expenditure	53.643	68.934	*World Development Indicators*
Duration				
No-party system	Length of time in years of duration of political system	2.405	4.685	Data collected by research team from *Keesings Contemporary Archives*; *Africa Confidential*; *Economist Intelligence Unit*
One-party system	ditto	3.415	5.551	ditto
Multiparty system	ditto	1.271	3.934	ditto
Neighbor average	Average level of reform among neighboring states, where 0 = no-party system, 1 = single-party system, and 3 = multiparty system	2.741	1.112	Data collected by research team from *Keesings Contemporary Archives*; *Africa Confidential*; *Economist Intelligence Unit*
1990–95	1 if 1990–95, 0 otherwise			

Note: All independent variables lagged by one year.

159

Appendix

Political Reform

The fiscal crisis of the states of late-century Africa, I have argued, led to a declining quality of public services and to increased predation by pubic officials, both of which sparked popular resentment and increasing demands for political reform. Within Africa, political reform was contagious, disseminating rapidly across national boundaries and into neighboring states. It was lent impetus from abroad, as Africa's creditors chided its authoritarian regimes. The power of finance rose sharply when the interests of Western foreign policymakers aligned with those of the fiscal technocrats with the end of the Cold War.

Table A.6 presents the variables employed to test this line of argument. Reform is marked by the movement from military to civilian regimes and from no- and single-party to multiparty systems among the latter. To analyze the determinants of such movements, I employ a conditional logit model (Table A.7).

As a result of this specification, several countries drop out of portions of the analysis, some – like Botswana – because they remained multiparty systems throughout the sample period; others – such as Swaziland – because they never reformed; some – such as the Democratic Republic of Congo – because they were "always" governed by a professional soldier; and still others – such as Tanzania – because they consistently remained under civilian rule.

Table A.7. Correlates of political reform, conditional logit

	Adoption of a Multiparty System				Adoption of a Civilian Regime			
	Coefficient (1)	P > t	Coefficient (2)	P > t	Coefficient (3)	P > t	Coefficient (4)	P > t
Income	0.000 (0.956)	0.344			0.001 (2.222)	0.042		
Urban population	0.071 (1.648)	0.116			−0.020 (−0.554)	0.585		
Literacy	−0.003 (−0.109)	0.915			−0.004 (−0.172)	0.867		
Modernization			0.218 (0.252)	0.807			0.393 −0.597	0.557
Petroleum	0.001 (0.909)	0.363	0.001 (0.832)	0.405	−0.002 (−1.393)	0.171	0.000 (−0.221)	0.825
Trade taxes	0.018 (1.308)	0.211	0.017 (1.343)	0.192	−0.033 (−2.767)	0.012	−0.029 (−2.204)	0.045

(continued)

Table A.7 (continued)

	Adoption of a Multiparty System				Adoption of a Civilian Regime			
	Coefficient (1)	P > t	Coefficient (2)	P > t	Coefficient (3)	P > t	Coefficient (4)	P > t
Business cycle	−14.782 (−1.987)	0.048	−14.523 (−1.983)	0.048	0.359 (0.060)	0.952	0.838 (−0.141)	0.888
Aid dependence	−0.002 (−0.369)	0.712	0.000 (0.004)	0.996	−0.008 (−1.246)	0.234	−0.010 (−1.992)	0.051
Duration								
No-party system	−0.124 (−2.588)	0.010	−0.094 (−2.132)	0.033	−0.246 (−5.023)	0	−0.256 (−5.641)	0.000
Single-party system	−0.100 (−2.898)	0.004	−0.082 (−2.407)	0.016	0.104 (2.396)	0.018	0.100 (2.277)	0.024
Neighbor average	0.328 (1.954)	0.054	0.358 (2.250)	0.025	0.545 (2.939)	0.006	0.596 (3.647)	0.000
1990–1995	1.938 (3.579)	0.003	2.292 (5.388)	0.000	0.741 (1.810)	0.074	0.643 (1.686)	0.094
Number of observations	980		728		728		675	

Note: t statistics in parentheses. Estimates derived from a conditional logistic model, grouped by country.

Appendix

As seen in Table A.7, the analysis suggests that political institutions in Africa exhibit historisis. As indicated by the coefficients on the duration variable, the longer a country has been subject to a no- or single-party system, the less likely it is to change to a multiparty system. The estimates also suggest a relationship between political reform and fiscal dearth. In the case of civilian regimes, declines in the growth rate of the advanced industrial nations ("business cycle") significantly and negatively correlate with increases in the likelihood of changing to a multiparty system; in the case of military governments, declines in "trade taxes" significantly and negatively relate to the likelihood of converting to a civilian form of government.

The coefficient on "urban population" suggests the role played by urban dwellers in the movement to multiparty systems; that on "income," the role played by the middle and upper classes in overturning military regimes. That protest diffused across political boundaries is confirmed by the positive and significant coefficient on "neighbor average," which provides a measure of the degree of political liberalization in neighboring states (see Table A.6).

Interestingly, aid dependence appears not to bear a statistically detectable relationship with the likelihood of change to a multiparty system; and in the movement to civilian regimes, the strength of its relationship varies depending upon the variables included or dropped from the analysis. More robust is

	Change in Probability	95% Confidence Interval	
Income			
From min to max	−0.057	−0.666	0.031
296 6,965			
Urban population			
From min to max	0.105	0	0.87
2.4 81.7			
Literacy			
From min to max	−0.049	0.543	0
17.1 100			
Petroleum	0.08	−0.052	0.858
From min to max			
0 6,574			
Trade taxes	0.044	0	0.443
From min to max			
.022 76.51			
Business cycle	−0.029	−0.294	0
From min to max			
−0.018 .052			
Aid dependence			
From min to max	−0.025	−0.352	0.034
0 513			
Duration of party system			
No-party system			
From min to max	−0.109	−0.782	0
0 25			
One-party system			
From min to max	−0.101	−0.731	0
0 25			
Neighbor average			
From min to max	0.024	−0.005	0.295
0 6			
1990–95			
From	0.048	0	0.383
0 1			

Note: Estimates derived from simulations of a probit that included country dummies. Consult Fernandez-Val. (2004), "Estimation of Structural Parameters and Marginal Effects in Binary Choice Panel Data Models with Fixed Effects," Cambridge, MA: Department of Economics, MIT.

Appendix

the relationship between the time dummy and the likelihood of reform: the coefficient on the variable "1990–95," which may capture the impact of the end of the Cold War, is positive in sign and statistically significant.

Table A.8 reports the magnitudes of the coefficients of equation 1 of Table A.7. The coefficient on the measure of duration under single-party rule suggests that those long subject to single-party rule, such as Tanzania, would be roughly 10% less likely to reform than would others, such as Kenya, whose experience with single-party rule was more limited. The data in Table A.8 also suggest that countries such as Rwanda or Burundi, where urban dwellers constitute less than 5% of the population, were 10% less likely to adopt multiparty rule than were those, such as Botswana or Cape Verde, where they composed over 60% of the population.

Political Disorder

The analysis of political disorder focused on the impact of three forces. The first was public revenues: When deprived of sufficient payments for the provision of governance, I argued, elites would use their power to pay themselves. They would veer from the equilibrium path, in the words of the fable, and behave in ways that would render citizens insecure. The second was political reform: When compelled to allow political opponents to organize in an effort to displace them, political elites, feeling

Table A.9. Variables pertaining to political disorder

	Measure	Mean	Standard Deviation	Source
Dependent Variable				
Militias	1 = Yes 0 = No	0.247	0.431	Data collected by research team from *Keesings Contemporary Archives Africa Confidential Economist Intelligence Unit*
Independent Variables				
Revenues	Central government's revenues as percent of GDP	18.489	0.382	*World Development Indicators*
Petroleum	Value of exports per capita in constant U.S. dollars	87.010	14.331	Data collected by research team from commercial sources
Party System				
No-party system	1 = Yes 0 = No	0.355	0.015	Data collected by research team from *Keesings Contemporary Archives Africa Confidential Economist Intelligence Unit*
One-party system	ditto	0.445	0.015	
Multiparty system	ditto	0.205	0.013	
Duration				
No-party system	Length of time in years of duration of political system	2.405	4.685	Data collected by research team from *Keesings Contemporary Archives Africa Confidential Economist Intelligence Unit*
One-party system	ditto	3.415	5.551	ditto
Multiparty system	ditto	1.271	3.934	ditto

Variable	Description			Source
Neighbor average	Number of neighboring states reporting militias or civil or international wars	1.514	1.953	Data collected by research team from *Keesings Contemporary Archives* *Africa Confidential* *Economist Intelligence Unit*
Privileged region	1 = yes 0 = no	0.891	0.331	Harvard research team
President from non-privileged region	1 = yes 0 = no	0.570	1.953	ditto
Period1	1 if 1970–74 0 otherwise			
Period2	1 if 1975–79 0 otherwise			
Period3	1 if 1980–84 0 otherwise			
Period4	1 if 1985–89 0 otherwise			
Time since last report	Count	5.993	6.235	
Instrumental Variables				
Business cycle	Weighted average growth rate of G7 economies	0.021	0.019	Data created by research team using data from *Penn World Tables Mark 5.6*
Trade taxes	Percentage central government revenues from taxes on trade	34.210	16.32	World Development Indicators
Revenues	Central government's revenues as percent of GDP			*World Development Indicators*
Two-year lag		19.272	9.871	
Three-year lag		19.100	9.618	

Note: All independent variables lagged one year, unless otherwise noted.

insecure, would increase the rate at which they would discount the future, thus fearing less the disorder that might be provoked by their predatory actions. The last was resource abundance: in an environment richly endowed with natural resources, the potential economic losses following state failure could readily be offset by using the power of the government to appropriate the deposits. In such a setting, political elites would more readily succumb to the temptation to deviate from the equilibrium path and to change from guardians to predators.

Table A.9 defines and describes the variable employed to test this argument and lists the sources from which they were taken. Table A.10 presents the coefficients derived from two models: A logit model applied to the pooled sample and a conditional logit model, which incorporates country-specific effects. I attempted to locate instruments that would enable me to correct for the impact of political disorder on public revenues, but I failed to do so. Table A.11 records first differences, calculated from the first equation in Table A.10, which provide measures of the magnitude of the coefficients.

The coefficients on "revenues" are of the sign anticipated but significant only in the first model. The difference in the estimates from the two models suggests that it is the quantity rather than changes in the quantity of public revenues that counts. Note the data in Table A.11 regarding the magnitude of the coefficients. In the case of "revenues," the data suggest that a shift from the level of revenues garnered in Sierra Leone

Table A.10. Changes in the probability of militias

	Pooled Model Coefficient		Conditional Logit Coefficient	
	(1)	P > t	(2)	P > t
Revenues	−0.039	0.061	−0.017	0.556
	(−2.04)		(−0.609)	
Petroleum	0.000	0.743	−0.001	0.727
	(−0.328)		(−0.349)	
No-party system	−0.459	0.246	−0.788	0.107
	(−1.166)		(−1.616)	
One-party system	−1.017	0.045	−2.166	0.000
	(−2.004)		(−4.071)	
Duration				
No-party system	0.096	0.006	−0.019	0.649
	(2.789)		(−0.455)	
One-party system	0.038	0.238	0.146	0.000
	(1.179)		(3.642)	
Multiparty system	−0.024	0.600	0.065	0.357
	(−0.524)		(0.920)	
Privileged region	1.403	0.014		
	(2.491)			
President from non-privileged region	−0.567	0.093	−0.807	0.043
	(−1.679)		(−2.027)	
Neighbor average	0.092	0.161	−0.052	0.552
	(1.401)		(−0.595)	
Period1	−1.504	0.000	−1.611	0.002
	(−3.526)		(−3.169)	
Period2	−0.914	0.009	−1.398	0.000
	(2.615)		(−3.565)	
Period3	−0.039	0.883	−0.076	0.819
	(−0.148)		(−0.228)	
Period4	−0.183	0.505	0.015	0.959
	(−0.667)		(0.051)	
Time since last report	−0.188	0.000	−0.017	0.497
	(−5.089)		(−0.68)	
Constant	−0.385	0.559		
	(−0.584)			
Number observations	1048		813	

Note: t statistics in parentheses. In equations 1 and 3, robust standard errors, clustered by country.

Table A.11. Magnitude of effects

	Pooled Model (First Differences)		
	Percent Change in Probability	95% Confidence Interval	
Revenues	−0.314	−0.634	−0.089
From min to max			
3.5 53.5			
Petroleum	−0.121	−0.897	0.403
From min to max			
0 6547.48			
No-party system	−0.070	−0.209	0.010
From 0 to 1			
One-party system	−0.111	−0.315	−0.007
From 0 to 1			
Duration			
No-party system	0.486	0.171	0.734
From min to max			
0 25			
One-party system	0.182	−0.056	0.548
From min to max			
0 25			
Multi-party system	−0.054	−0.351	0.312
From min to max			
0 25			
Privileged region	0.231	−0.006	0.428
From 0 to 1			
President from non-privileged region	−0.072	−0.232	0.006
From 0 to 1			
Neighbor average	0.191	−0.047	0.518
From 0 to 1			
Period1	−0.137	−0.353	−0.030
From 0 to 1			
Period2	−0.103	−0.268	−0.017
From 0 to 1			
Period3	0.005	−0.071	0.103
From 0 to 1			
Period4	−0.023	−0.114	0.054
From 0 to 1			
Time since last report	−0.382	−0.708	−0.127
From min to max			
0 25			

Appendix

in the mid-1980s to that in Botswana in the same period would be associated with a 30% reduction in the likelihood of state failure. Given that political disorder is likely to depress the level of public revenues, these estimates are likely to be biased downward.

The coefficients for "petroleum," a measure of natural resource endowments, offer little evidence of a relationship between either differences or changes in the level of the value of natural resources and the likelihood of reports of militias. Insofar as the coefficient on "privileged region" (equation 1) incorporates the effect of natural resource endowments, its sign and significance does offer evidence in favor of such a relationship.[7] The coefficient on "president from non-privileged region" is negative and significant in both equations, suggesting that political tensions decline when the poorer region gains control of the state. As seen in Table A.11, countries containing a "privileged region" are 23% more likely to experience state failure. Having a president from a non-privileged region reduces the likelihood by 7 percentage points; the estimate is imprecise, however.

The two sets of findings – that having to do with regional differences and that with the origins of heads of state – warrant

---

[7] The variable "privileged region" should be viewed as an imperfect first step toward capturing *within* country variation. Better is the rapidly increasing use of geographic information systems, as by Buhaug, H. and G. Gates, "The Geography of Civil War," *Journal of Peace Research* 39(4): 417–33.

Appendix

additional discussion. Acemoglu and Robinson (2001) and Azam and Mesnard (2003) view politics as centering on redistribution. Economic inequality – class, in the case of Acemoglu and Robinson and region, in the case of Azam and Mesnard – animates threats and the use of power. In response to threats and to forestall violence, those with wealth may offer to share it; but in the absence of credible means to commit themselves to fulfill such promises, such offers may well be discounted. What makes such promises credible, they argue, is the restructuring of institutions. In Acemoglu and Robinson (2001), the restructuring takes the form of empowering the poor, as by broadening the franchise or increasing the powers of popular assemblies. In the context of Africa, the lodging of executive power in the hands of poorer regions may play an analogous role to empowerment of the lower classes in industrial states. The greater credibility of pledges to use the power of the state to redistribute the wealth of the nation may help to account for the negative relationship between our measure of disorder and the holding of the presidency by the poorer regions of the nation; by the same token, the negative relationship may provide evidence in support of their arguments.

The last of the "theoretical" variables is the party system. A change to a competitive party system, I have argued, leads to an increase in the level of political risk. Most relevant, then, are the coefficients of Table A.10 that are based on within-country changes; both the coefficients on the

Appendix

"no-party" and "one-party" are negative, and the latter is highly significant. The estimates of the magnitude of the coefficients (Table A.11) are based on equation 1; because they pertain to differences between rather than to changes in levels, they can have but little bearing on this discussion.

The control variables also yield coefficients of interest. Those of "Period1" and "Period2" (1970–74 and 1975–79, respectively) are significantly lower than those of "Period5" (1990–95, the reference category), thus offering evidence of an increase in the likelihood of disorder over time. The estimates in Table A.11 indicate that reports of militias were 10 to 14% less likely in the 1970s than in the 1990s. As seen in the coefficient to "neighbor average," countries whose neighbors experienced more violence were more likely to experience disorder, although the coefficient is not statistically significant. The data in Table A.11 suggest the magnitude of the effect: A country such as Mauritius, being an island and therefore isolated from unruly neighbors, would be roughly 20% less likely to experience political disorder than, say, Zaire in 1994, which bordered six neighbors engulfed in political conflict.

The estimates remain robust to the inclusion of additional control variables. These include the standard "modernization" variables: measures of education, income, and urbanization. They also include measures of shocks: economic shocks, such as terms of trade or growth shocks; climatic shocks, such as droughts; and political shocks, such as national elections. They include as well such standard controls as population, to capture the size of the country; and such non-standard controls, as a measure of the extent to which ethnic groups sprawl across national borders.

In conclusion, I would draw attention to the "duration" variables. In any given year and for any given party system, these variables indicate the number of years that the system has been in place. When the duration variables are excluded from the models, the coefficients on the party system dummies fail to behave in a systematic manner. When they are included, the coefficients behave in ways that are meaningful and are highly robust to the inclusion of other variables and to the choice of model. Why should this be the case? The pattern may be a statistical artifact, and therefore of little significance, or it may suggest something about the nature of political institutions and therefore be important. I continue to be puzzled – and tantalized – by this finding, but I leave the issue unresolved while drawing it to the attention of others.

Bibliography

Acemoglu, D., and J. A. Robinson (2001). "A Theory of Political Transitions." *American Economic Review* 91(4): 938–63.

Achebe, C. (1975). *Things Fall Apart*. New York: Fawcett Crest.

Adam, C. S., and S. A. O'Connell (1999). "Aid, Taxation, and Development in Sub-Saharan Africa." *Economics and Politics* 11(3): 225–54.

Alexander, M. (2007). *Is Poverty to Be Blamed for Civil Wars?* Cambridge, MA: Paper submitted to gov. 2782, Spring Term. Department of Government, Harvard University.

Allen, C. (1989). Benin. In *Benin, The Congo, Burkina Faso: Economics, Politics, and Society*. Edited by C. Allen, M. S. Radu, K. Somerville, and J. Baxter. London and New York: Pinter Publishers: 1–137.

Anguka, J. (1998). *Absolute Power: The Ouko Murder Mystery*. London: Pen Press.

Asprey, R. B. (1986). *Frederick the Great*. New York: Ticknor and Fields.

Axelrod, R. (1985). *The Evolution of Cooperation*. New York: Basic Books.

Azam, J.-P. (1994). "How to Pay for Peace? A Theoretical Framework with Reference to African Countries," *Public Choice* 83(1–2): 173–84.

———. (2001). "The Redistributive State and Conflicts in Africa." *The Journal of Peace Research* 38(4): 429–44.

———. (2007). The Political Geography of Redistribution. Chapter 6 in *The Political Economy of Economic Growth in Africa, 1960–2000: An Analytic Survey*. Edited by B. Ndulu, P. Collier, R. H. Bates, and S. O'Connell. Cambridge, U.K.: Cambridge University Press.

Azam, J.-P., and A. Mesnard (2003). "Civil War and the Social Contract." *Public Choice* 115(3–4): 455–75.

Banks, A. (1999). *Cross-National Times Series Data Archive*. Binghamton, NY: Center for Social Analysis, State University of New York at Binghamton.

Bibliography

Barkan, J. D. (1976). "Further Reassessment of 'Conventional Wisdom': Political Knowledge and Voting Behavior in Rural Kenya." *American Political Science Review* 70(2): 452–55.

———. (1986). *Politics and the Peasantry in Kenya*. Nairobi: Institute for Development Studies, University of Kenya.

Baron, D., and J. Ferejohn (1989). "Bargaining in Legislatures." *American Political Science Review* 83(4): 1181–1206.

Barro, R., and J.-W. Lee (1993). "International Comparisons of Educational Attainment." *NBER Working Paper 4349*, April.

Bartlett, R. (1993). *The Making of Europe: Conquest, Colonization, and Cultural Change, 950–1350*. Princeton, NJ: Princeton University Press.

Bates, R. H. (1976). *Rural Responses to Industrialization*. New Haven and London: Yale University Press.

———. (1989). *Beyond the Miracle of the Market*. Cambridge, U.K.: Cambridge University Press.

Bates, R. H., A. Greif, et al. (2002). "Organizing Violence." *Journal of Conflict Resolution* 46(5): 599–628.

Bates, R. H., and I. Yackolev (2002). Ethnicity in Africa. In *The Role of Social Capital in Development*. Edited by C. Grootaert and T. van Bastelaer. New York: Cambridge University Press.

Bates, R., D. Epstein, et al. (2006). *Political Instability of Task Force Report, Phase IV Findings*. McLean, VA: SAIC.

Bayart, J.-F. (1989). Cameroon. In *Contemporary West African States*. Edited by Donal B. Cruise O'Brien, John Dunn, and Richard Rathbone. London: Oxford University Press.

Bazenguissa-Ganga, R. (2003). The Spread of Political Violence in Congo-Brazzaville. In *Readings in African Politics*. Edited by T. Young. Oxford: James Currey.

Beck, N., J. Katz, et al. (1998). "Taking Time Seriously: Time-Series-Cross-Section Aanalysis with a Binary Dependent Variable." *American Journal of Political Science* 42(4): 1260–88.

Birmingham, D. (2002). Angola. In *A History of Postcolonial Lusophone Africa*. Edited by P. Chabal. London: Hurst & Company: 138–84.

Bloch, M. (1970). *Feudal Society*. Chicago: University of Chicago Press.

Blumenthal, E. (1982). "Zaire: Rapport sur sa Credibilite Financiere Internationale." *La Revue Nouvelle* 77(November 11): 360–78.

Boone, C. (1990). *Merchant Capital and the Roots of State Power*. New York: Cambridge University Press.

Bibliography

————. (2003). *Political Topographies of the African State: Rural Authority and Institutional Choice.* Cambridge, U.K.: Cambridge University Press.

Brass, P., ed. (1985). *Ethnic Groups and the State.* London: Croom, Helm.

Bueno de Mesquita, B., A. Smith, et al. (2003). *The Logic of Political Survival.* Cambridge, MA: The MIT Press.

Buhaug, H., and S. Gates (2002). "The Geography of Civil War." *Journal of Peace Research* 39(4): 417–33.

Buhaug, H. and J. K. Rod (2006). "Local Determinants of African Civil Wars, 1970–2001." *Political Geography* 25: 315–35.

Buijtenhuijs, R. (1989). Chad. In *Contemporary West African States.* Edited by John Dunn, Donal B. Cruise O'Brien, and Richard Rathbone. Cambridge, U.K.: Cambridge University Press.

Burdette, M. (1988). *Zambia.* Boulder, CO: Westview.

Carneiro, R. L. (1970). "A Theory of the Origin of the State." *Science* 169(3946): 733–38.

Cederman, L.-E., and L. Girardin (2007). "Beyond Fractionalization: Mapping Ethnicity on Nationalist Insurgencies." *American Political Science Review* 101(1): 173–85.

Chabal, P. (2002). *A History of Postcolonial Lusophone Africa.* London: Hurst and Company.

Cohen, M. (1974). *Urban Policy and Political Conflict in Africa: A Study of the Ivory Coast.* Chicago: University of Chicago Press.

Collier, P. (2000). Doing Well Out of Civil War. In *Greed and Grievance: Economic Agendas in Civil War.* Edited by M. Berdal and D. Malone. Boulder, CO: Lynne Rienner.

Collier, P., A. Hoeffler, et al., eds. (2003). *Breaking the Conflict Trap: Civil War and Development Policy.* Washington, DC: The World Bank.

Collier, P., and A. Hoeffler (2004). "Greed and Grievance in Civil Wars." *Oxford Economic Papers,* New Series 56(4): 563–95.

Collier, P., and S. O'Connell (2007). Opportunities, Choices and Syndromes. Chapter 2 in *The Political Economy of Economic Growth in Africa, 1960–2000.* Edited by B. Ndulu, P. Collier, R. H. Bates, and S. O'Connell. Cambridge, U.K.: Cambridge University Press.

Dahl, R. (1971). *Polyarchy.* New Haven: Yale University Press.

Daily Nation. "Constituency Review: Laikipia District." July 16, 2002, pp. 11–14.

de Waal, A. (1991). *Evil Days: Thirty Years of War and Famine in Ethiopia.* New York: Human Rights Watch.

Bibliography

de Waal, A., and A. H. A. Salam (2004). Islamism, State Power, and *Jihad* in Sudan. In *Islamism and Its Enemies in the Horn of Africa*. Edited by A. de Waal. Bloomington, IN, Indiana University Press.

Dianga, J. W. (2002). *Kenya, 1982: The Atttempted Coup.* London: Penn Press.

Dietrich, C. (2000). Inventory of Formal Diamond Miniing in Angola. In *Angola's War Economy*. Edited by J. Cilliers and C. Dietrich. Pretoria, South Africa: Institute for Security Studies.

Dumont, R. (1962). *L'Afrique Noire est Mal Partie*. Paris: Editions Seuil.

———. (1966) *False Start in Africa*. New York: Praeger.

Dudley, B. (1982). *An Introduction to Nigerian Government and Politics.* Bloomington, IN: Indiana University Press.

Dunning, T. (2004). "Conditioning the Effects of Aid: Cold War Politics, Donor Credibility, and Democracy in Africa." *International Organization* 58(2): 409–23.

Easterly, W., and R. Levine (1997). "Africa's Growth Tragedy: Policies and Ethnic Divisions." *Quarterly Journal of Economics* 112(4): 1203–50.

Elliott, C., ed. (1971). *Constraints on the Economic Development of Zambia.* Nairobi: Oxford University Press.

Ellis, S. (1999). *The Making of Anarchy*. New York: New York University Press.

Emizet, K. N. F. (1998). "Confronting Leaders at the Apex of the State: The Growth of the Unofficial Economy of the Congo." *African Studies Review* 41(1): 99–137.

Epstein, D. L., R. Bates, et al. (2006). "Democratic Transitions." *American Journal of Political Science* 59(3): 551–69.

Evans, P., T. Skocpol, and D. Rueschmeyer (1985). *Bringing the State Back In.* Cambridge, U.K.: Cambridge University Press.

Fanon, F. (1963). *The Wretched of the Earth*. New York: Presence Africaine.

Fearon, J. D. (2004). "Why Do Some Civil Wars Last So Much Longer than Others?" *Journal of Peace Research* 41(3): 275–301.

———. (2005). "Primary Commodities Exports and Civil War." *Journal of Conflict Resolution* 49(4): 483–507.

Fearon, J. D., and D. Laitin (2003). "Ethnicity, Insurgency and Civil War." *American Political Science Review* 97(1): 75–90.

Finance Magazine. "Kalenjin Liberation Army." Septemberr 15, 1992, pp. 20–6.

Fortes, M. (1958). Introduction. In *The Developmental Cycle in Domestic Groups*. Edited by J. Goody. Cambridge, U.K.: Cambridge University Press.

Fortes, M., and E. E. Evans-Pritchard, eds. (1987). *African Political Systems.* New York: KPI in association with the International African Institute.

Bibliography

Fowler, R. R. (2000). "Report of the Panel of Experts on Violations of Security Council Sanctions Against UNITA." New York: S. Council, The United Nations.

Fratkin, E., E. A. Roth, et al. (1994). Introduction. In *African Pastoralist Systems*. Edited by E. Fratkin, E. A. Roth and K. A. Galvin. Boulder, CO: Lynne Rienner.

Gboyega, A. (1997). Nigeria: Conflict Unresolved. In *Governance as Conflict Management*. Edited by I. W. Zartman. Washington, DC: Brookings Institution Press.

Geddes, B. (2003). *Paradigms and Sand Castles*. Ann Arbor: University of Michigan Press.

Gertzel, C., C. Baylies, et al., eds. (1984). *The Dynamics of the One-Party State in Zambia*. Manchester: U.K.: University of Manchester Press.

Goldstone, J., R. Bates, et al. (2005). *A Global Forecasting Model of Political Instability*. McClean, VA: State Failure Task Force, SAIC.

Gould, D. (1980). *Bureaucratic Corruption and Underdevelopment in the Third World: The Case of Zaire*. London: Pergamon Press.

Groseclose, T., and J. M. Snyder (1996). "Buying Supermajorities." *American Political Science Review* 90(2): 303–15.

Hansen, H. B., and M. Twaddle (1995). Uganda: The Advent of No-Party Democracy. In *Democracy and Political Change in Sub-Saharan Africa*. Edited by J. Wiseman. London: Routledge.

Hayward, F. (1976). "A Reassessment of Conventional Wisdom about the Informed Public: National Political Information in Ghana." *American Political Science Review* 70(2): 917–41.

Hayward, F. M., and J. D. Kandeh (1987). Perspectives on Twenty-Five Years of Elections in Sierra Leone. In *Elections in Independent Africa*. Edited by F. M. Hayward. Boulder, CO: Westview Press.

Hegre, H. (2003). Disentangling democracy and development as determinants of armed conflict. Paper presented at the annual meeting of the International Studies Association, Portland, Oregon.

———. (2004). "The Duration and Termination of Civil War." *Journal of Peace Research* 41(3): 243–52.

Hegre, H., S. Gates, et al. (2001). "Toward a Democratic Civil Peace? Democracy, Political Change and Civil War, 1816–1992." *American Political Science Review* 95(1): 33–48.

Heilbrunn, J. (1993). "Social Origins of National Conferences in Benin and Togo." *Journal of Modern African Studies* 31(2): 277–99.

Bibliography

———. (1997). Togo: The National Conference and Stalled Reform. In *Political Reform in Francophone West Africa*. Edited by J. F. Clark and D. E. Gardiner. Boulder, CO: Westview Press.

Helleiner, G. (1966). *Peasant Agriculture, Government, and Economic Growth in Nigeria*. Homewood, IL: R. D. Irwin.

Hempstone, S. (1997). *Rogue Ambassador*. Sewanee, TN: University of the South Press.

Herbst, J. (2000). "Economic Incentives, Natural Resources and Conflict in Afruca." *Journal of African Economies* 9(3): 270–94.

Herbst, J. (2000). *States and Power in Africa*. Princeton, NJ: Princeton University Press.

Heston, A., R. Summers, et al. (2002, October). *Penn World Tables Version 6.1.* Philadelphia: Center for International Comparisons, University of Pennsylvania.

Hirshleifer, J. (2001). *The Dark Side of the Force*. Cambridge, U.K.: Cambridge University Press.

———. (1995). Theorizing about Conflict. In *Handbook of Defense Economics*. Edited by K. Hartley and T. Sandler. New York: Elsevier.

Huntington, S. P. (1991). *The Third Wave*. Norman, OK: Oklahoma University Press.

Jalata, A. (2005). *Oromo and Ethiopia: State Formation and Environmental Conflict, 1868–2004*. Trenton, NJ: Red Sea Press.

Johnson, D. H. (1995). The Sudan People's Liberation Army and the Problem of Factionalism. In *African Guerillas*. Edited by C. Clapham. Oxford, U.K.: James Currey.

———. (2003). *The Root Causes of Sudan's Civil War*. Bloomington, IN: Indiana University Press.

Jones, B. D. (1999). Civil War, the Peace Process, and Genocide in Rwanda. In *Civil Wars in Africa*. Edited by T. M. Ali and R. O. Matthews. Montreal: McGill-Queens Press.

———. (1999). Military Intervention in Rwanda's Two Wars: Partisanship and Indifference. In *Civil Wars, Insecurity, and Intervention*. Edited by B. F. Walters and J. Snyder. New York: Columbia University Press.

———. (2001). *Peacemaking in Rwanda: The Dynamics of Failure*. Boulder, CO: Lynne Rienner.

Kabwegyere, T. (1995). *The Politics of State Formation and Destruction in Uganda*. Kampala, Fountain Publishers.

Kakwenzire, J., and D. Kamukama (2000). The Development and Consolidation of Extremist Forces in Rwanda. In *The Path of a Genocide: The Rwanda*

Bibliography

Crisis from Uganda to Zaire. Edited by H. Adelman and A. Suhrke. London: Transaction Publishers.

Kalyvas, S. (2006). *The Logic of Violence in Civil War.* Cambridge, U.K.: Cambridge University Press.

Kaplan, R. D. (1994). "The Coming Anarchy." *The Atlantic Monthly* 273(February 2): 44–76.

Kasara, K. (2007). "Tax Me If You Can." *American Political Science Review* 101(1): 159–72.

Kasfir, N. (1976). *The Shrinking Political Arena.* Berkeley and Los Angeles: University of California Press.

Kasozi, A. B. K. (1994). *The Social Origins of Violence in Uganda, 1964–1985.* Montreal: McGill-Queen's University Press.

Keen, D. (1998). "The Economic Functions of Violence in Civil War." *Adelphi Paper 320.* Oxford, U.K.: International Institute for Strategic Studies.

———. (2000). Incentives and Disincentives for Violence. In *Greed and Grievance: Economic Agendas in Civil Wars.* Edited by M. Berdal and D. Malone. Boulder, CO: Lynne Rienner.

———. (2001). The Political Economy of War. In *War and Underdevelopment: The Economic and Social Consequences of Conflict,* Vol. 1. Edited by F. Stewart, V. Fitzgerald and Associates. Oxford, U.K.: Oxford University Press.

Kenyatta, J. (1953). *Facing Mount Kenya.* London: Secker and Warburg.

Khadiagala, G. M. (1995). State Collapse and Reconstruction in Uganda. In *Collapsed States.* Edited by I. W. Zartman. Boulder, CO: Lynne Rienner.

Kimenyi, M. S., and N. Ndung'u (2005). Sporadic Ethnic Violence: Why Has Kenya Not Experienced a Full Blown Civil War? In *Understanding Civil War: Evidence and Analysis, Volume 1 (Africa).* Edited by P. Collier and N. Sambanis. Washington, DC: The World Bank.

King, G., J. Honeker, et al. (2001). "Analyzing Incomplete Political Science Data: An Alternative Algorithm for Multiple Imputation." *American Political Science Review* 95(1): 49–69.

Kpundeh, S. J. (1995). *Politics and Corruption in Africa: A Case Study of Sierra Leone.* New York: University Press of America.

Kramer, G. H. (1983). "Electoral Politics in the Zero-Sum Society." *Social Science Working Paper 472.* Pasadena, CA: Division of Humanities and Social Science, California Institute of Technology.

Kriger, N. (2003). *Guerrilla Veterans in Post-War Zimbabwe: Symbolic and Violent Politics, 1980–1987.* Cambridge, U.K.: Cambridge University Press.

Larmer, M. (2006). "A Little Bit Like a Volcano": *The United Progressive Party and Resistance to One-Party Rule in Zambia,* 1964–1980. Typescript.

Bibliography

Leakey, L. S. B. (1977). *The Southern Kikuyu before 1903*. London: Academic Press.

Lemarchand, R. (1981). "Chad: The Roots of Chaos." *Current History* 80(470): 414–18, 436–38.

———. (1993). Burundi in Camparative Perspective. In *The Politics of Ethnic Conflict Regulation*. Edited by J. McGarry and B. O'Leary. London: Routledge.

———. (2003). The Democratic Republic of the Congo: From Failure to Potential Reconstruction. In *State Failure and State Weakness in a Time of Terror*. Edited by R. I. Rotberg. Cambridge, MA, and Washington, DC: The World Peace Foundation/Brookings Institution: 29–70.

Levine, V. T. (1986). Leadership and Regime Changes in Perspective. In *The Political Economy of Cameroon*. Edited by M. G. Schatzberg and I. W. Zartman. New York: Praeger.

Lewis, H. (2001). *A Galla Monarchy*. Madison, WI: University of Wisconsin Press.

Little, I. M. D., T. Scitovsky, et al. (1970). *Industry and Trade in Some Developing Countries*. Oxford, U.K.: Oxford University Press.

MacGaffey, J. (1991). *The Real Economy of Zaire*. Philadelphia: University of Pennsylvania Press.

Magaloni, B. (2006). *Voting for Autocracy: Hegemonic Party Survival and Its Demise in Mexico*. New York: Cambridge University Press.

Mamdani, M. (2001). *When Victims Become Killers*. Princeton, NJ: Princeton University Press.

Mansfield, E., and J. Snyder (1995). "Democratization and War." *Foreign Affairs* 74(3): 79–97.

Marcus, H. G. (2002). *A History of Ethiopia*. Berkeley and Los Angeles: University of Los Angeles Press.

Marshall, M. G., and K. Jaggers (2000). *Polity IV Project: Political Regime Characteristics and Transitions, 1800–1999 Dataset Users' Manual*. College Park, MD: CIDCM, University of Maryland.

May, R. (2003). Internal Dimensions of Warfare in Chad. In *Readings in African Politics*. Edited by T. Young. Oxford: James Currey.

Mbithi, P. M., and C. Barnes (1975). *The Spontaneous Settlement Problem in Kenya*. Kampala, Uganda: East African Literature Bureau.

Meillassoux, C. (1981). *Maidens, Meal, and Money*. Cambridge, U.K.: Cambridge University Press.

Meredith, M. (2005). *The State of Africa: A History of Fifty Years of Independence*. London: Free Press.

Bibliography

Murshed, S. M., and S. Gates (2003). Spatial-Horizontal Inequality and the Maoist Insurgency in Nepal. Paper commissioned by The Department for International Development, UK. London.

Musah, A.-F. (2000). A Country Under Siege: State Decay and Corporate Military Intervention in Sierra Leone. In *Mercenaries: An African Security Dilemma*. Edited by A.-F. Musah and J. K. Fayemi. London: Pluto Press.

Musah, A.-F., and J. K. Fayemi (2000). Africa in Search of Security. In *Mercenaries: An African Security Dilemma*. Edited by A.-F. Musah and J. K. Fayemi. London: Pluto Press.

Mwakikagile, G. (2001). *Ethnic Politics in Kenya and Nigeria*. Huntington, NY: Nova Science Publishers.

National Council of Churches of Kenya. (1992). *The Cursed Arrow*. Nairobi: NCCK.

Ndulu, B., P. Collier, et al. (2007). *The Political Economy of Economic Growth in Africa, 1960–2000*, 2 vols. Cambridge, U.K.: Cambridge University Press.

Ngaruko, F., and J. D. Nkurunziza (2000). "An Economic Interpretation of Conflict in Burundi." *Journal of African Economies* 9(3): 370–409.

Nnoli, O. (1998). Ethnic Conflicts in Africa: A Comparative Analysis. In *Ethnic Conflict in Africa*. Edited by O. Nnoli. Dakar, Senegal: Codesria.

Nolutshungu, S. C. (1996). *Limits of Anarchy*. Charlottesville: University Press of Virginia.

Nzongola-Ntalaja, G. (2002). *The Congo from Leopold to Kabila*. London: Zed Books.

———. (2004). The Politics of Citizenship in the DRC. Paper prepared for the annual *International Conference*. Edinburgh: University of Edinburgh.

Oquaye, M. (1980). *Politics in Ghana, 1972–1979*. Accra, Ghana: Tornado Publications.

Ottaway, M. (1999). *Africa's New Leaders*. Washington, DC: Carnegie Endowment for International Peace.

Otunnu, O. (2000). An Historical Analysis of the Invasion of the Rwanda Patriotic Army. In *The Path of a Genocide: The Rwanda Crisis from Uganda to Zaire*. Edited by H. Adelman and A. Suhrke. London: Transaction Publishers.

Ould-Abdallah, A. (2000). *Burundi on the Brink, 1993–1995*. Washington, DC: United States Institute of Peace Press.

Pech, K. (2000). The Hand of War: Mercenaries in the Former Zaire 1996–97. In *Mercenaries: An African Security Dilemma*. Edited by A.-F. Musah and J. K. Fayemi. London: Pluto Press.

Please, S. (1984). *The Hobbled Giant*. Boulder, CO: Westview.

Bibliography

Polanyi, K. (1991). *Dahomey and the Slave Trade.* New York: AMS Press.

Popkin, S. L. (1979). *The Rational Peasant.* Berkeley and Los Angeles: University of California Press.

Prunier, G. (1998). *The Rwanda Crisis: History of a Genocide.* London: Hurst.

Rapley, J. (1993). *Ivoirien Capitalism: African Entrepreneurs in Côte d' Ivoire.* Boulder, CO: Lynne Rienner.

Reno, W. (1995). *Corruption and State Politics in Sierra Leone.* Cambridge, U.K.: Cambridge University Press.

———. (2000). Shadow States and the Political Economy of Civil Wars. In *Greed and Grievance: Economic Agendas in Civil Wars.* Edited by M. Berdal and D. Malone. Boulder, CO: Lynne Riennner.

———. (2003). Sierra Leone: Warfare in a Post-State Society. In *State Failure and State Weakness in a Time of Terror.* Edited by R. I. Rotberg. Cambridge and Washington, DC: The World Peace Foundation/Brookings Institution: 71–100.

Republic of Kenya, Parliamentary Select Committee. (1992). *Report of the Parliamentary Select Committee to Investigate Ethnic Clashes in Western and Other Parts of Kenya.* Nairobi: Kenya Parliament.

Reyna, S. P. (1990). *Wars Without End: The Political Economy of a Precolonial African State.* Hanover: University Press of New England for the University of New Hampshire.

Ricardo, D. (1821). *On the Principles of Political Economy and Taxation.* London: John Murray.

Richards, P. (1995). Rebellion in Liberia and Sierra Leone: A Crisis of Youth? In *Crisis in Africa.* Edited by O. Furley. London: I. B. Tauris.

Robinson, P. (1994). "The National Conference Phenomenon in Francophone Africa." *Comparative Studies in Society and History* 36(3): 575–610.

Ross, M. L. (2004). "How Does Natural Resource Wealth Influence Civil Wars? Evidence from Thirteen Cases." *International Organization* 49(4): 508–37.

Rubin, D. B. (1996). "Multiple Imputation after 18+ Years (with discussion)." *Journal of the American Statistical Association* 91(434): 473–89.

Rutten, M. (2001). "Fresh Killings": The Njoro and Laikipia Violence in the 1997 Kenyan Elections Aftermath. In *Out for the Count: The 1997 General Elections and Prospects for Violence in Kenya.* Edited by M. Rutten, A. Mazrui, and F. Gignon. Kampala, Uganda: Fountain Publishers.

Sachs, J., and A. Warner (1995). "Economic Reform and the Process of Global Integration." *Brookings Papers on Economic Activity* (1): 1–118.

Sahlins, M. D. (1961). "The Segmentary Lineage: An Organization of Predatory Expansion." *American Anthropologist* 63(2): 322–45.

Bibliography

———. (1968). *Tribesmen*. Englewood Cliffs, NJ: Prentice-Hall.

———. (1971). Tribal Economies. In *Economic Development and Social Change*. Edited by G. Dalton. Garden City, NY: Natural History Press for the American Museum of Natural History: 43–61.

Salih, M. A. M., and J. Markakis. (1998). *Ethnicity and State in Eastern Africa*. Uppsala, Sweden: Nordiska Afrikainstutel.

Sambanis, N., and H. Hegre (2006). "Sensitivity Analysis of Empirical Results on Civil War Onset." *Journal of Conflict Resolution* 50(4): 508–35.

Schafer, J. L. (1997). *Imputation of Missing Covariates in Multivariate Linear Mixed Model*. University Park, PA: Department of Statistics, The Pennsylvania State University.

Schatz, S. P. (1977). *Nigerian Capitalism*. Berkeley and Los Angeles: University of California Press.

Schumpeter, J. A. (1950). *Capitalism, Socialism and Democracy*. New York: Harper & Row.

Scott, J. C. (1976). *The Moral Economy of the Peasant*. New Haven and London: Yale University Press.

Smillee, I., L. Giberie, et al. (2000). *The Heart of the Matter: Sierra Leone, Diamonds, and Human Security*. Ottowa: Partnership Africa-Canada.

Snyder, J. (2000). *From Voting to Violence*. New York: W. W. Norton.

Snyder, R. (2006). "Does Lootable Wealth Breed Disorder? A Political Economy of Extraction Framework." *Comparative Political Studies* 39(8): 943–68.

Snyder, R., and R. Bhavani (2005). "Diamonds, Blood, and Taxes: A Revenue-Centered Framework for Explaining Political Order." *The Journal of Conflict Resolution* 49(4): 563–97.

Stevenson, R. F. (1968). *Population and Political Systems in Tropical Africa*. New York: Columbia University Press.

Szeftel, M. (1978). Conflict, Spoils, and Class Formation in Zambia. Ph.D. Dissertation. Manchester, U.K.: University of Manchester Press.

Tangri, R. (1999). *The Politics of Patronage in Africa: Parastatls, Privatizaton, and Private Enterprise*. Trenton, NJ: Africa World Press.

Thom, W. G. (1999). "Congo-Zaire's 1996–1997 Civil War in the Context of Evolving Patterns of Military Conflict in Africa in the Era of Independence." *The Journal of Conflict Studies* 19(2): 93–123.

Timmer, C. P. (1969). "The Turnip, the New Husbandry, and the English Agricultural Revolution." *Quarterly Journal of Economics* 83(2): 375–96.

Turner, V. (1957). *Schism and Continuity in an African Society*. Manchester, U.K.: University of Manchester Press on behalf of the Rhodes-Livingstone Institute.

Bibliography

Vansina, J. (1966). *Kingdoms of the Savanna*. Madison: University of Wisconsin Press.

Waller, R., and N. W. Sobania (1994). Historical Perspectives. In *African Pastoralist Systems*. Edited by E. Fratkin, K. A. Galvin, and E. A. Roth. Boulder, CO: Lynne Rienner.

Weber, M. (1958). Politics as a Vocation. In *From Max Weber*. Edited by H. H. Gerth and C. W. Mills. New York: Oxford University Press.

Weiner, M. (1978). *Sons of the Soil: Migration and Ethnic Conflict in India*. Princeton, NJ: Princeton University Press.

Weinstein, J. (2007). *Inside Rebellion*. Cambridge, U.K.: Cambridge University Press.

Weiss, H. (1995). Zaire: Collapsed Society, Surviving State, Future Policy. In *Collapsed States*. Edited by I. W. Zartman. Boulder, CO: Lynne Rienner.

Wilks, I. (1975). *Asante in the Nineteenth Century*. Cambridge, U.K.: Cambridge University Press.

World Bank. (1981). *Accelerated Development in Sub-Saharan Africa: An Agenda for Action*. Washington, DC: The World Bank.

———. (1989). *Sub-Saharan Africa: From Crisis to Sustainable Growth*. Washington, DC: The World Bank.

———. (1991). *Governance and Development*. Washington, DC: The World Bank.

———. (2006). *World Development Indicators 2006*. Washington, DC: The World Bank.

Wrigley, C. (1996). *Kingship and the State, The Buganda Dynasty*. New York and London: Cambridge University Press.

Zakaria, F. (1997). "The Rise of Illiberal Democracy." *Foreign Affairs* 76(November–December): 22–43.

Index

Index

Index

Index

Index

Printed in the United States
by Baker & Taylor Publisher Services